Soppy

◙ SQUARE PEG

Published by Square Peg 2015

2 4 6 8 10 9 7 5 3

First published in Great Britain in 2015 by
Square Peg
Vintage Books
Penguin Random House, 20 Vauxhall Bridge Road,
London SW1V 2SA
www.vintage-books.co.uk

Addresses for companies within The Random House Group Limited can be found at:
www.randomhouse.co.uk/offices.htm

The Random House Group Limited Reg. No. 954009

A CIP catalogue record for this book is available from the British Library

ISBN 9780224101066

The Random House Group Limited supports the Forest Stewardship Council® (FSC®), the leading international forest-certification organisation. Our books carrying the FSC label are printed on FSC certified paper. FSC is the only forest-certification scheme supported by the leading environmental organisations, including Greenpeace. Our paper procurement policy can be found at www.randomhouse.co.uk/environment

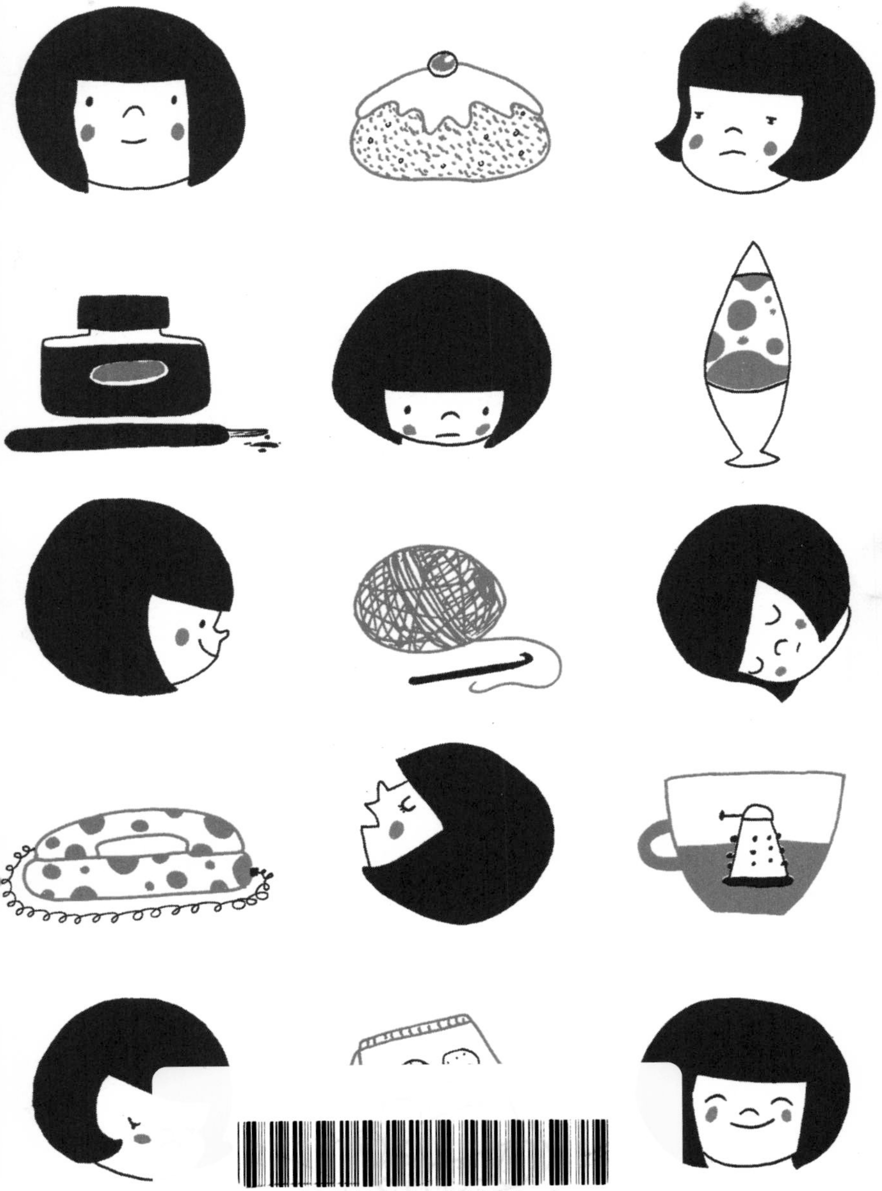

4000000115110 1

Philippa Rice is an artist who works in
a number of different mediums including
comics, illustration, animation, model-making
and crochet. Her other works include
the collage based webcomic, *My Cardboard Life*
and her stop-motion animated characters.
Philippa grew up in London and now she
lives in Nottingham with illustrator Luke Pearson.

for Luke

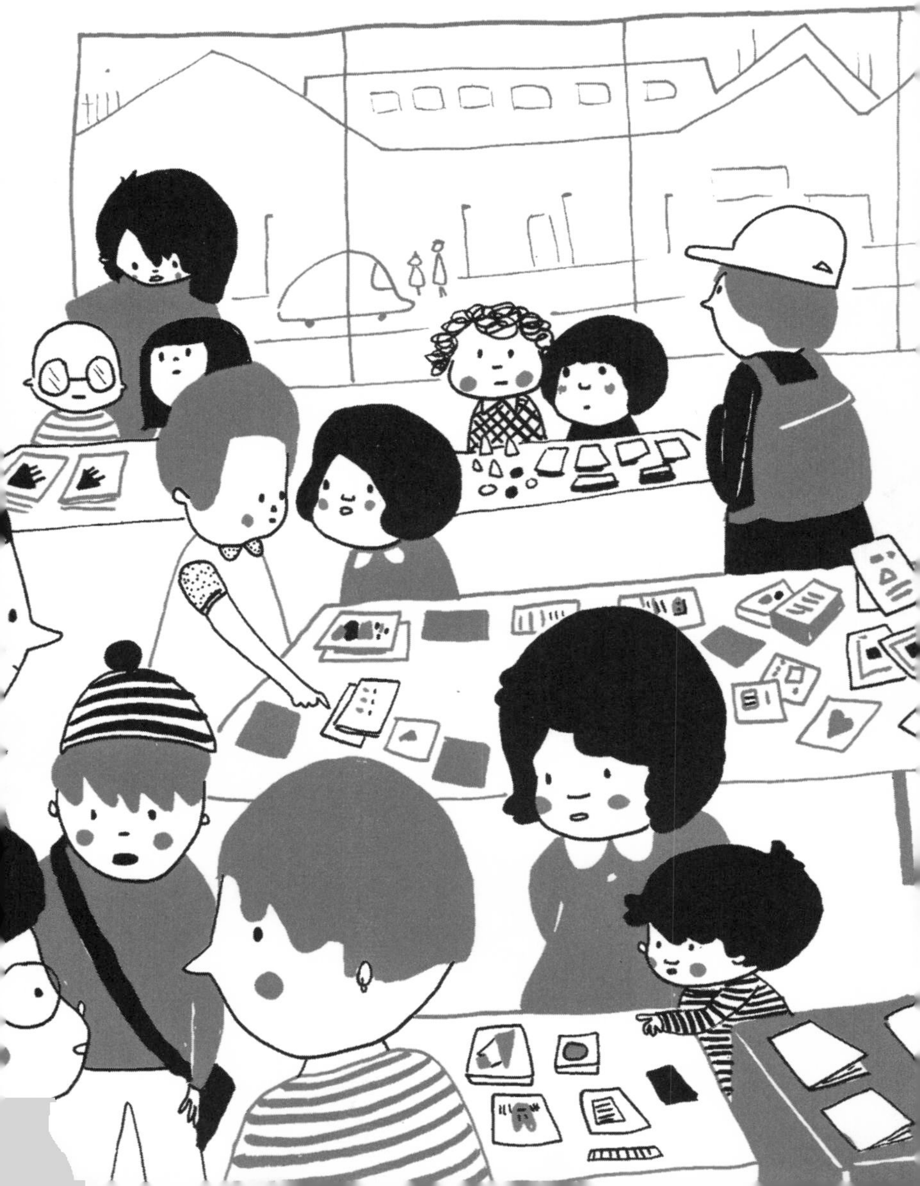

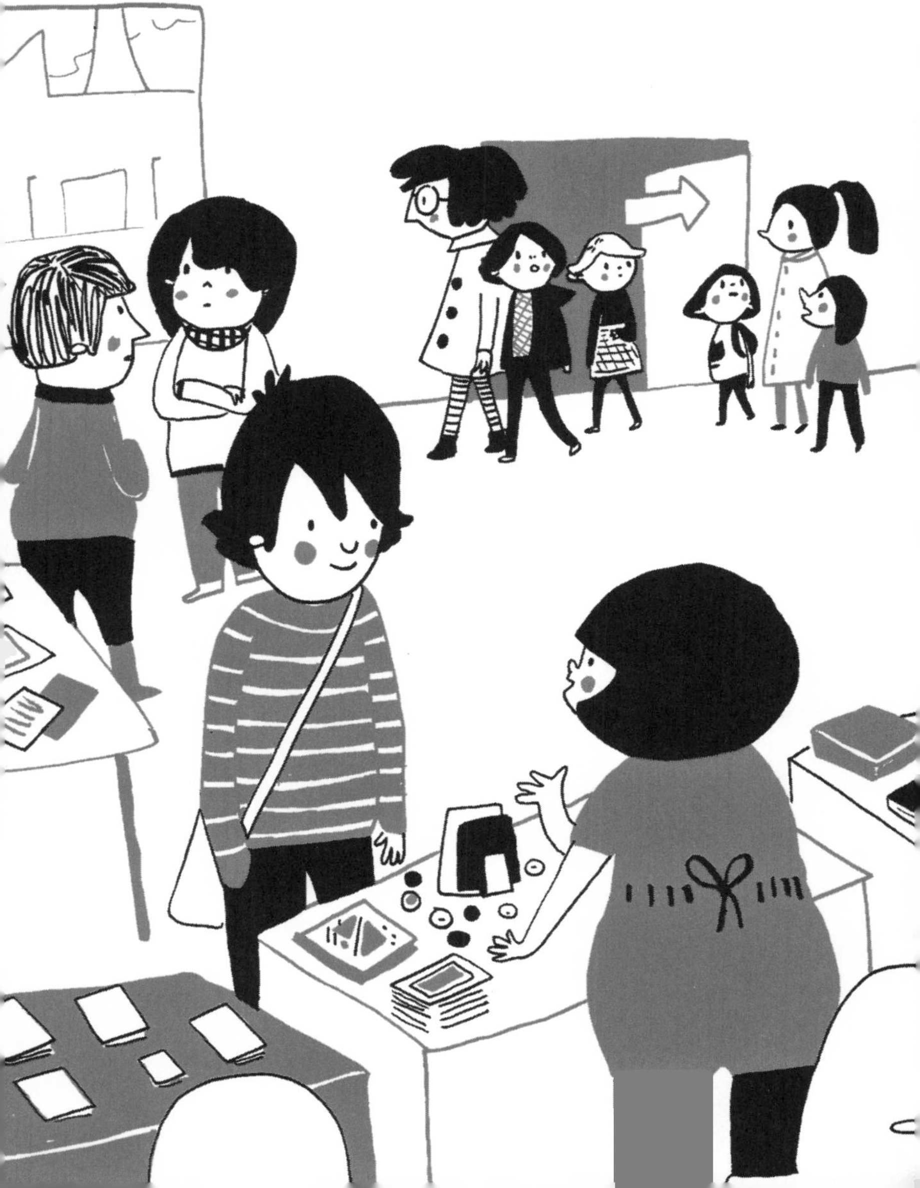

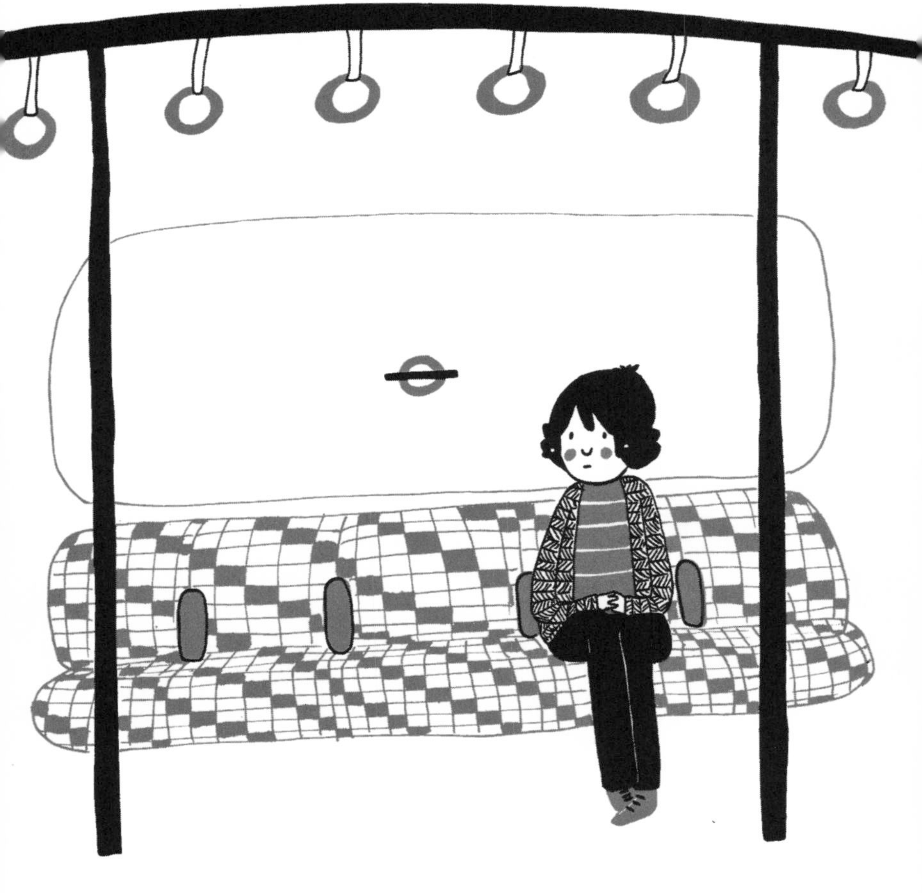

OPEN

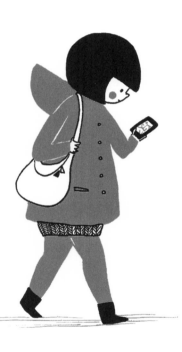

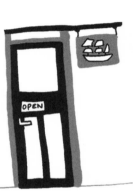

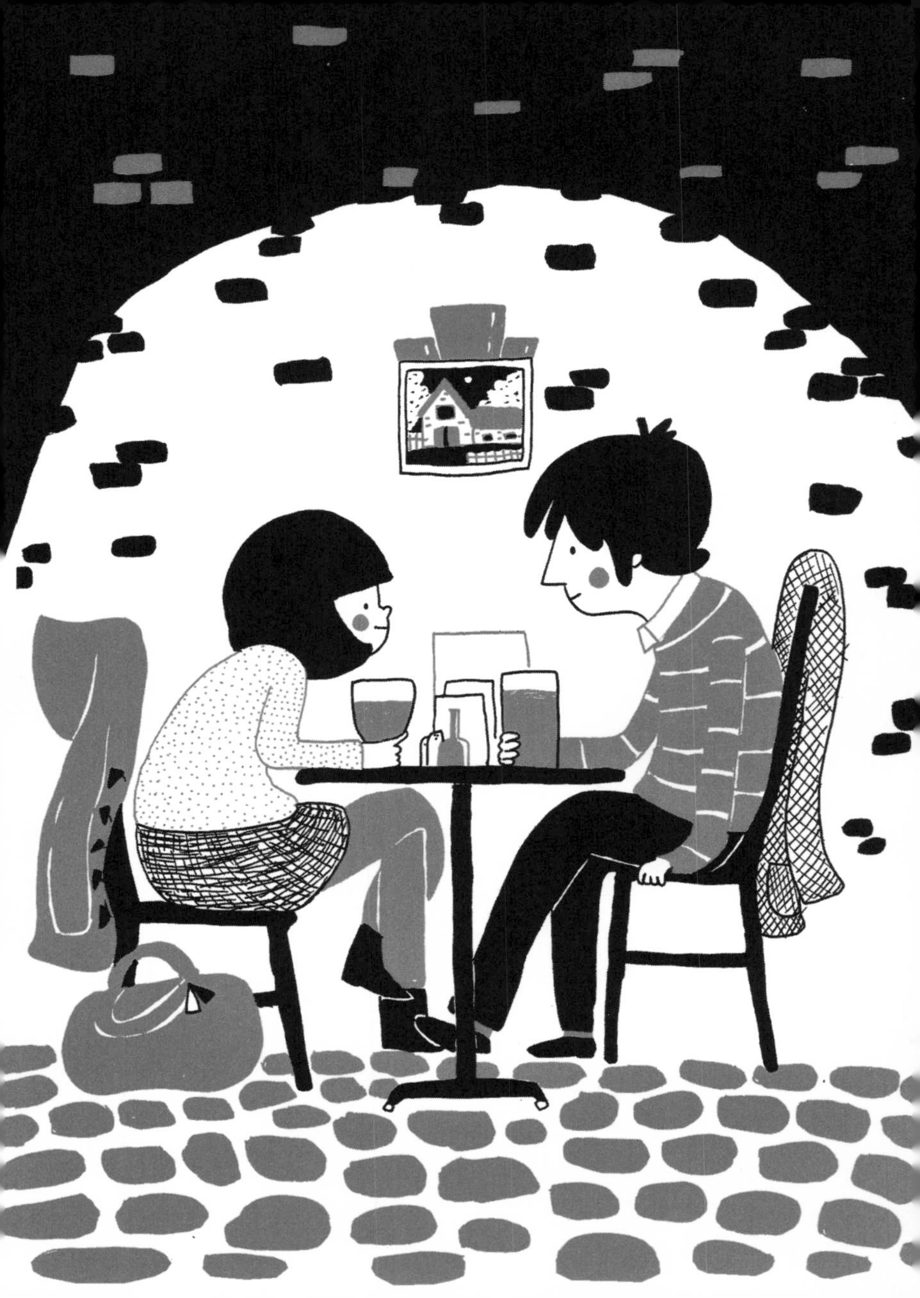

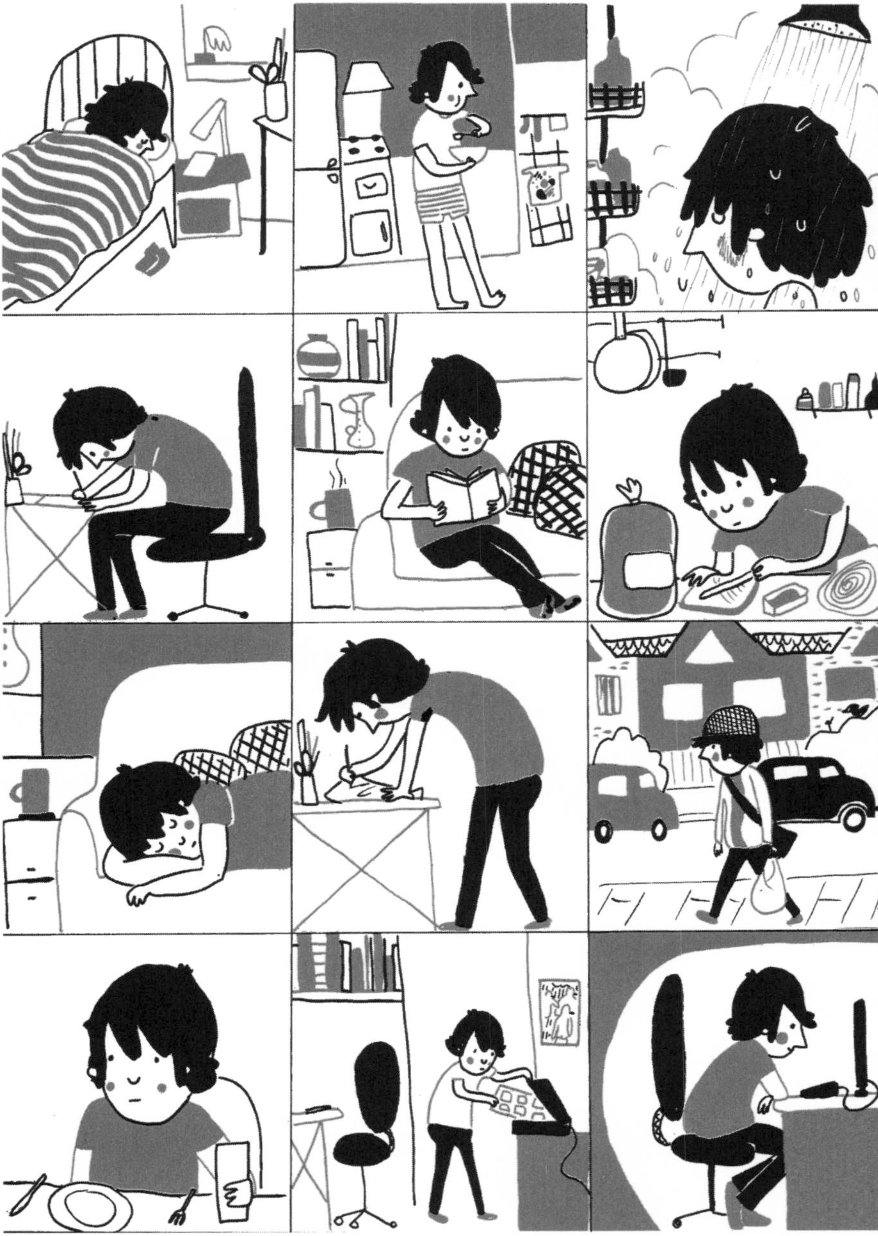

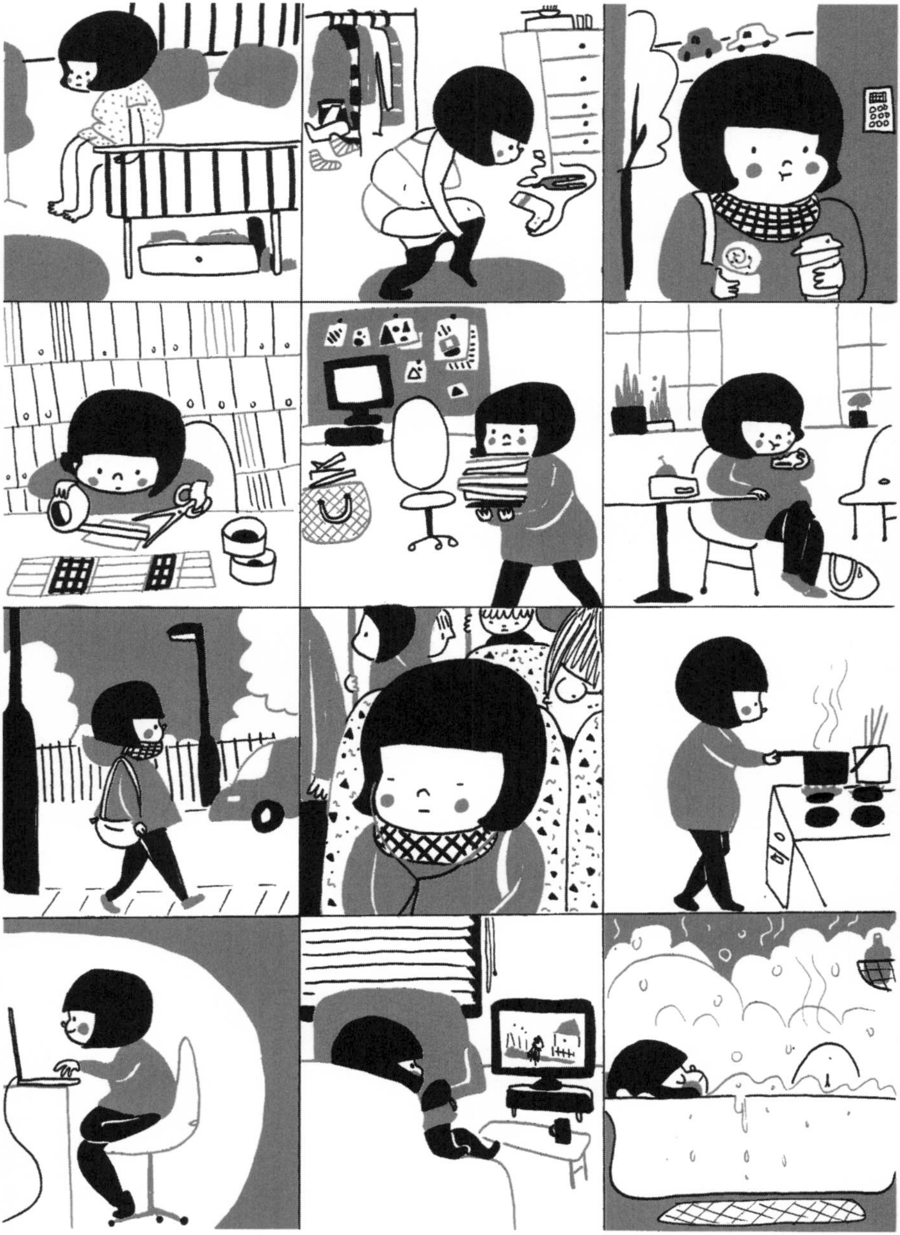

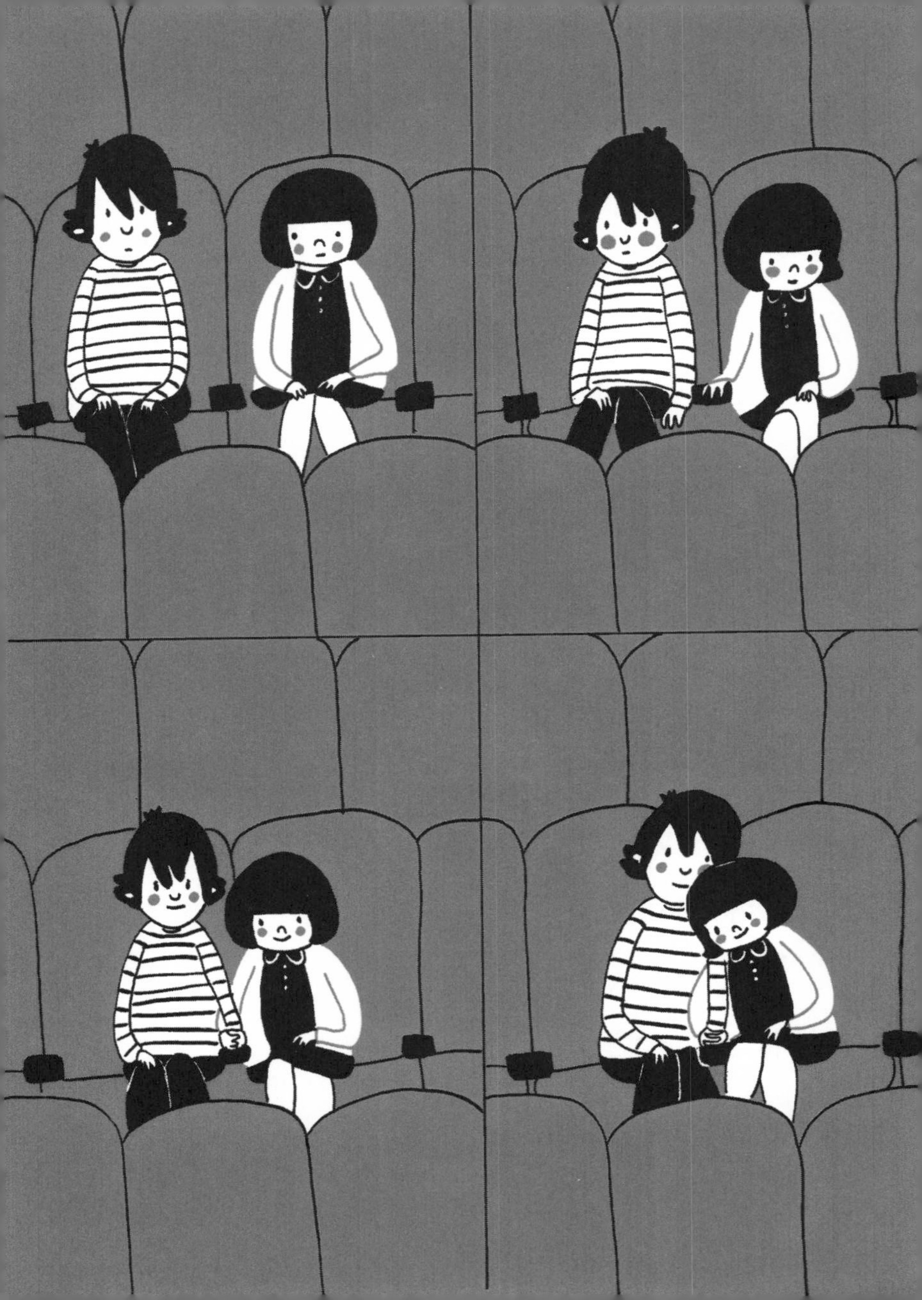

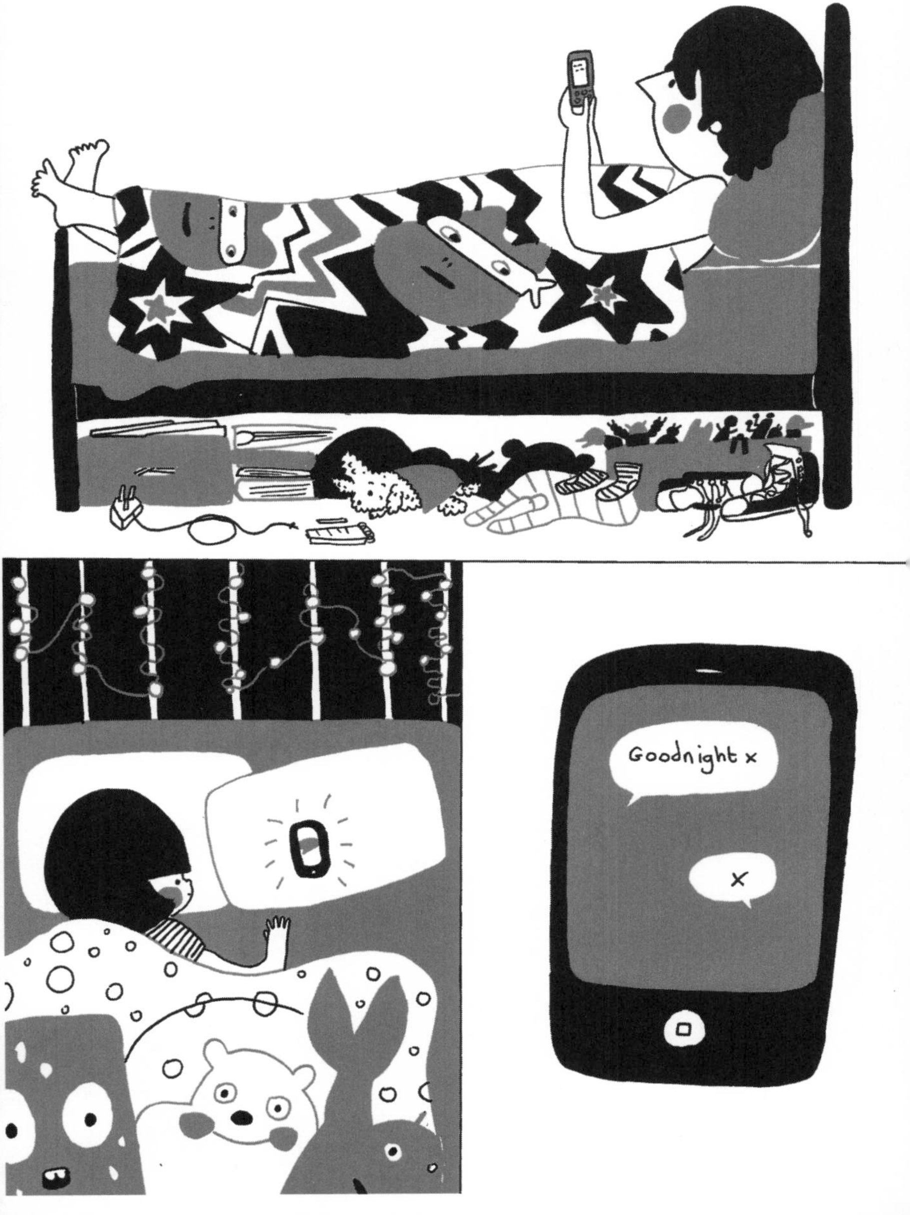
Goodnight x
x

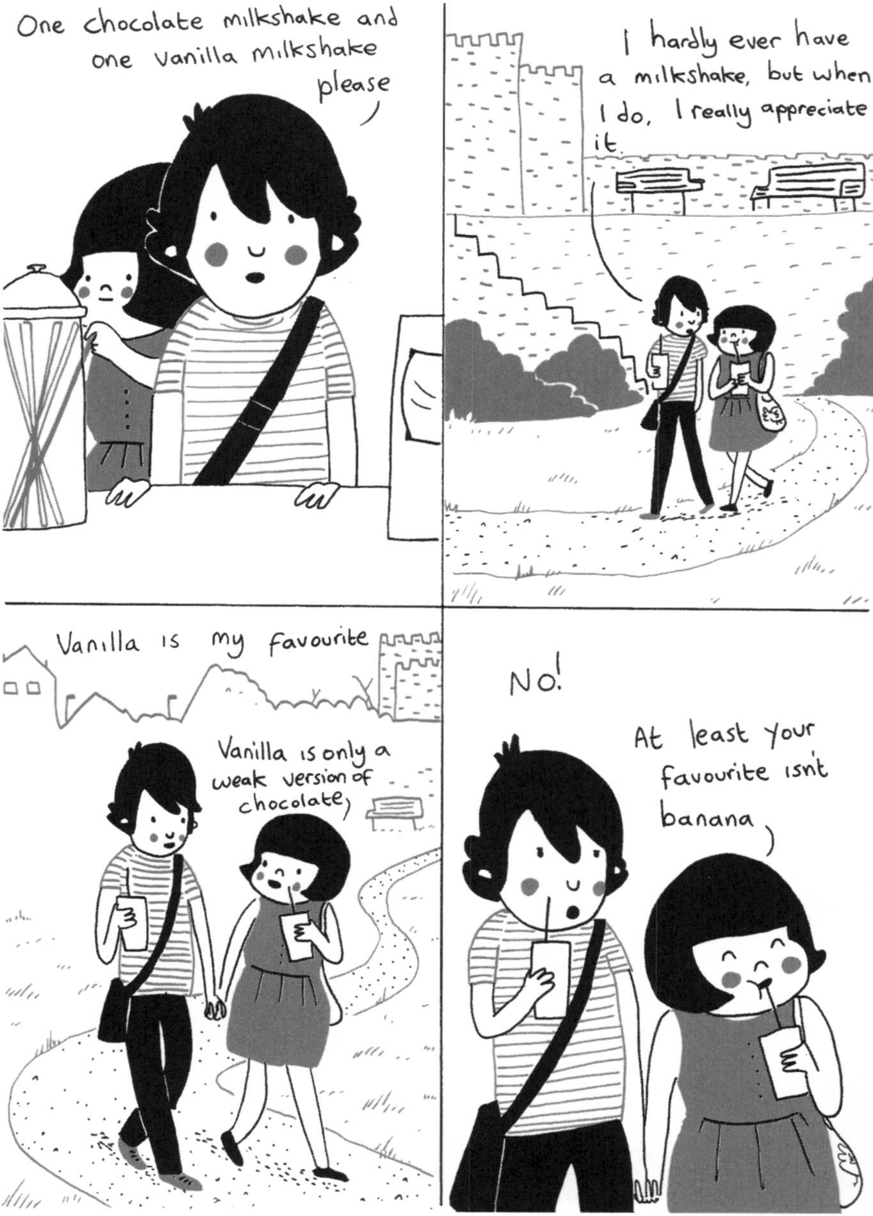
One chocolate milkshake and one vanilla milkshake please
I hardly ever have a milkshake, but when I do, I really appreciate it.
Vanilla is my favourite
Vanilla is only a weak version of chocolate
No!
At least your favourite isn't banana

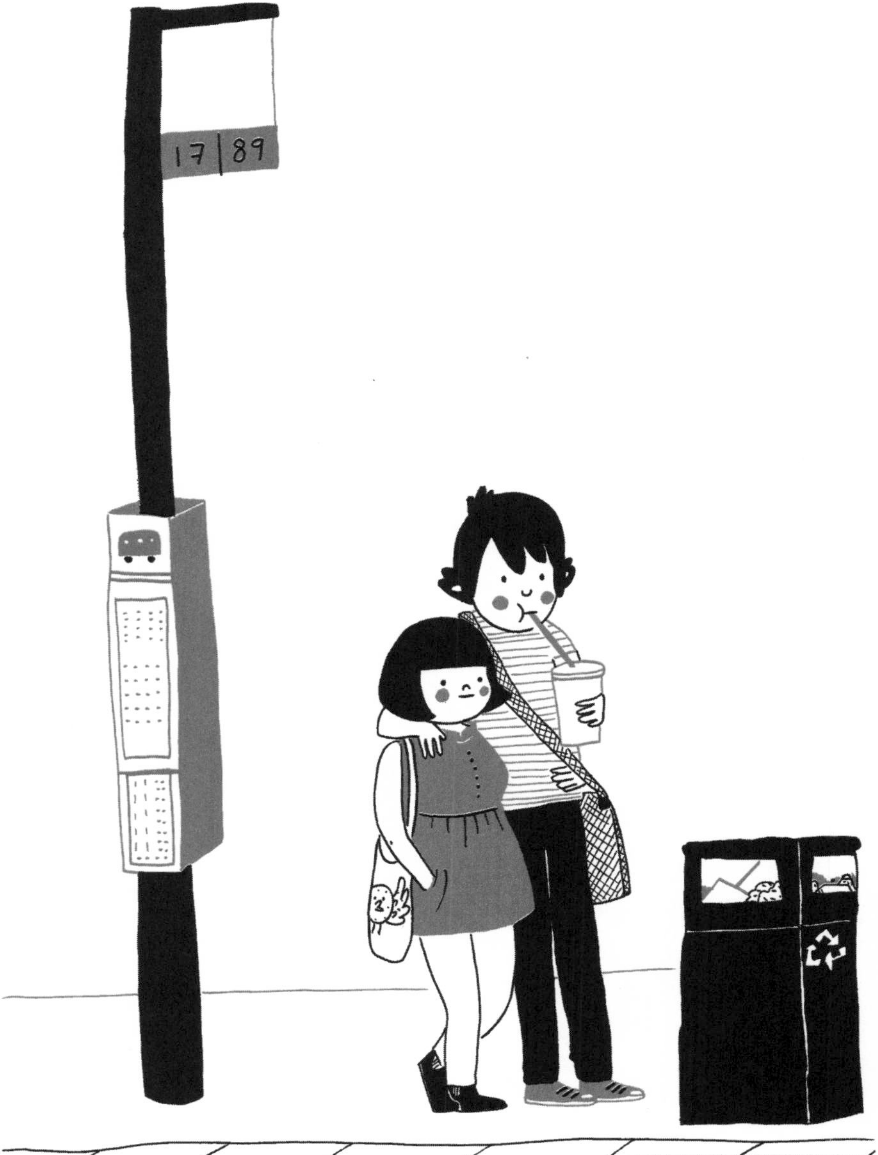
17 | 89

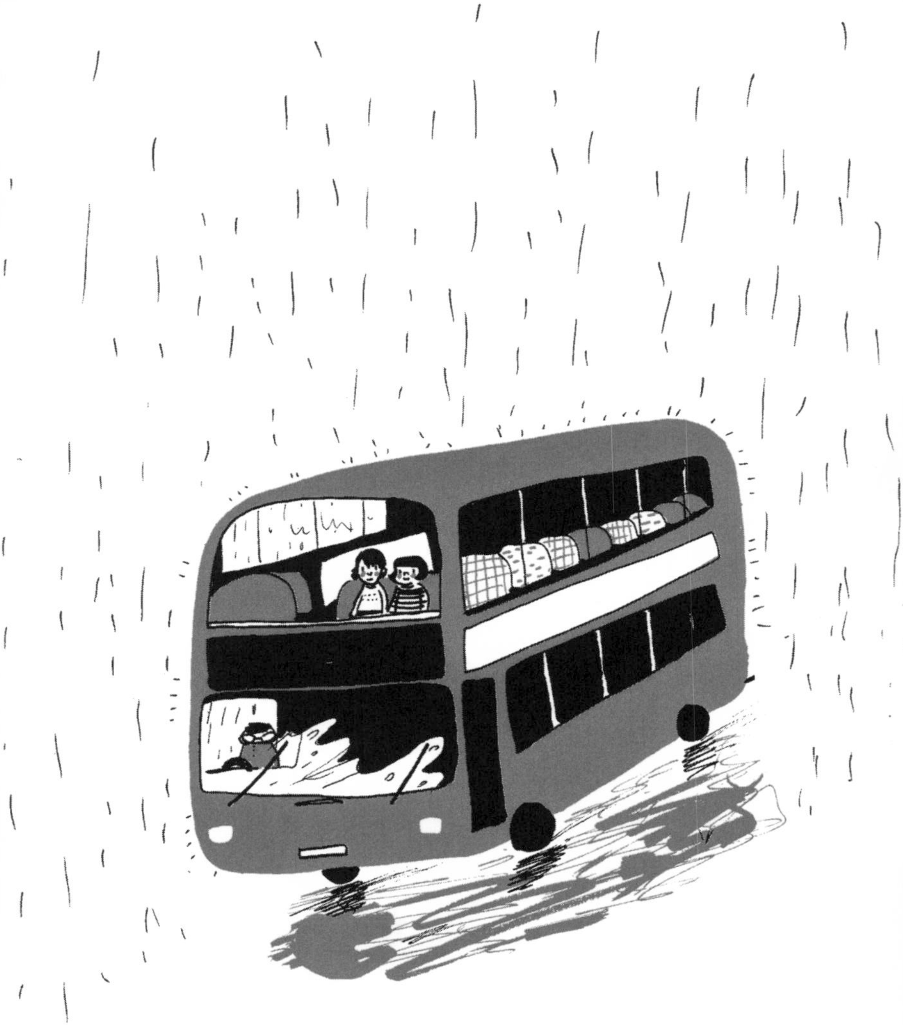

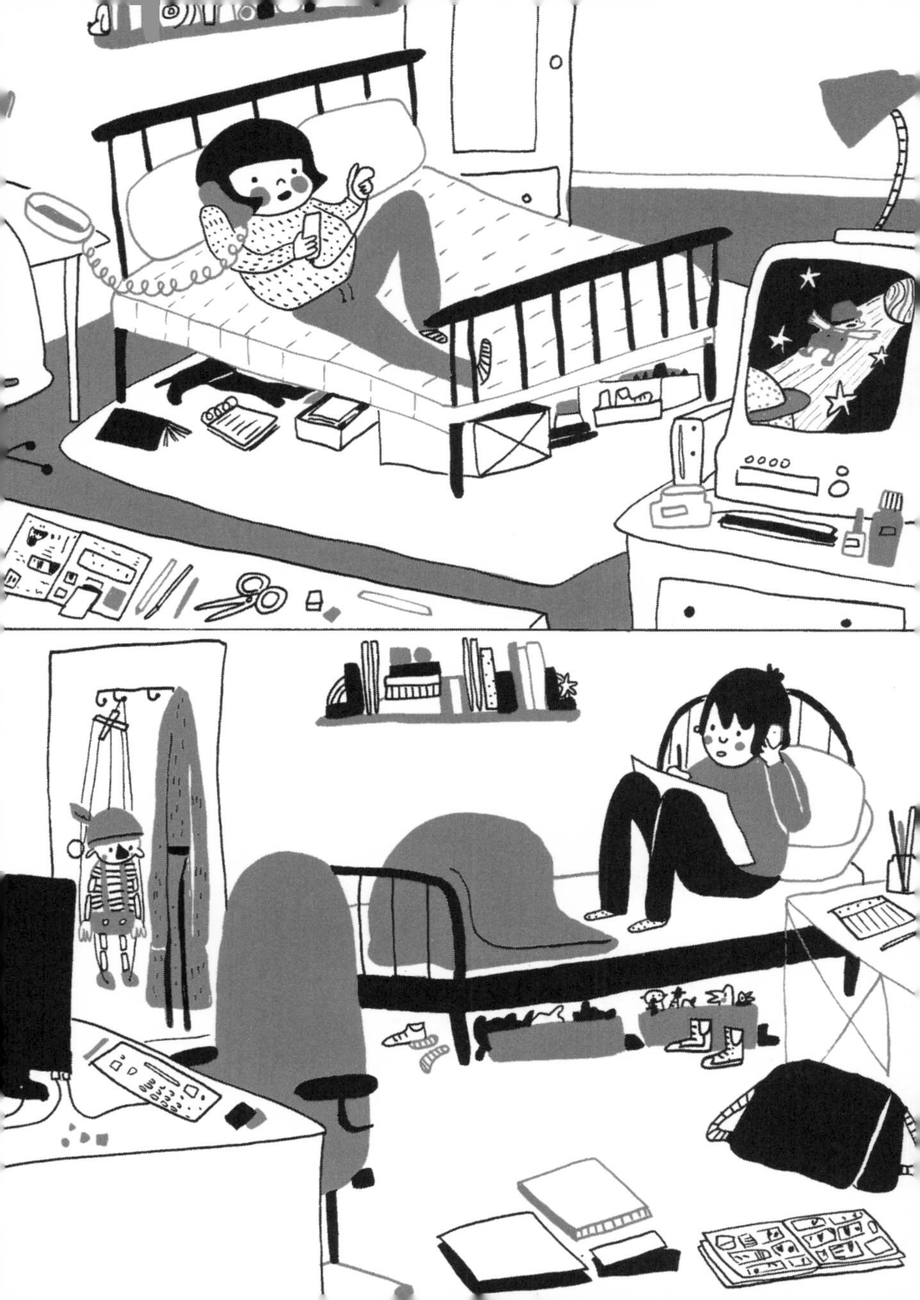

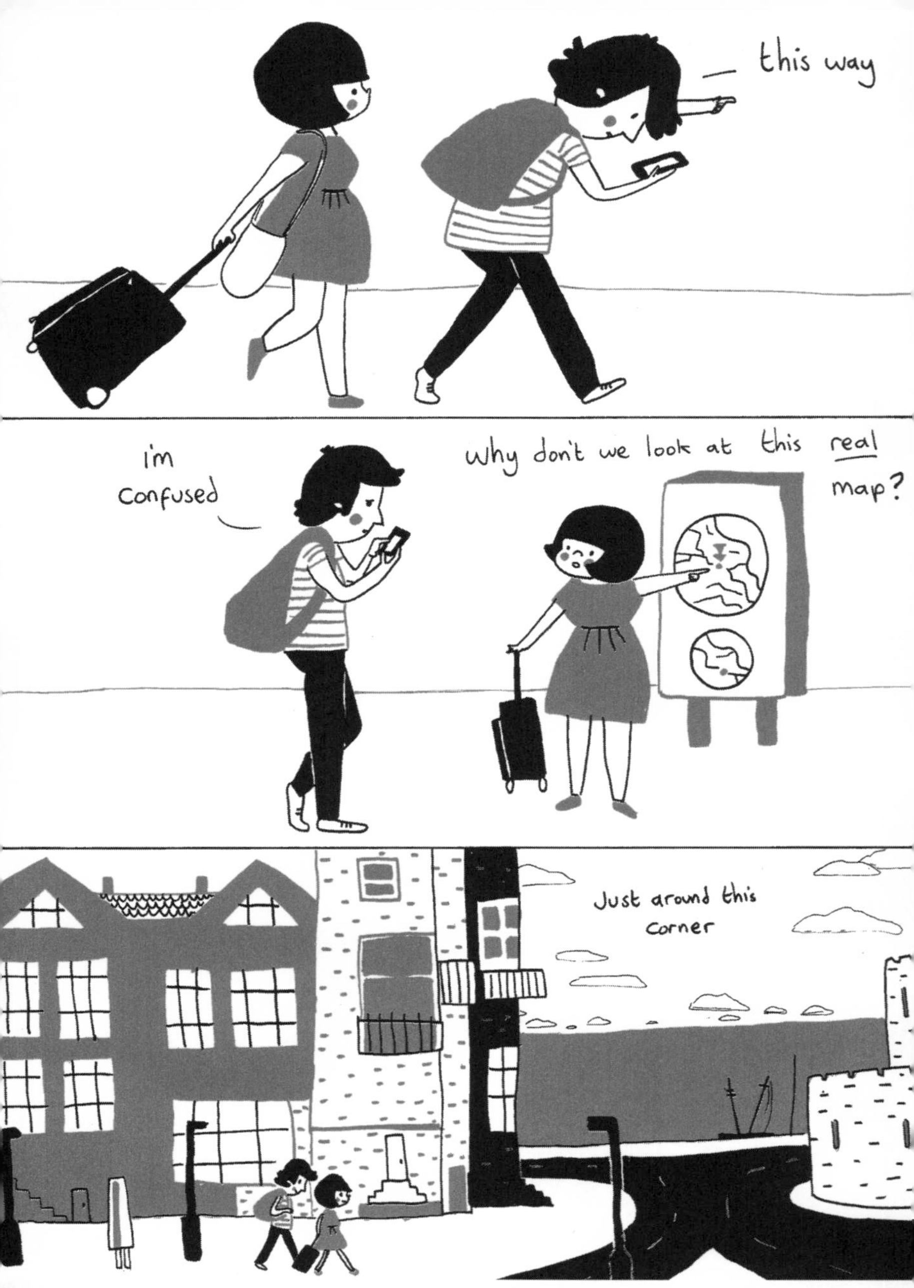
this way
i'm confused
why don't we look at this real map?
Just around this corner

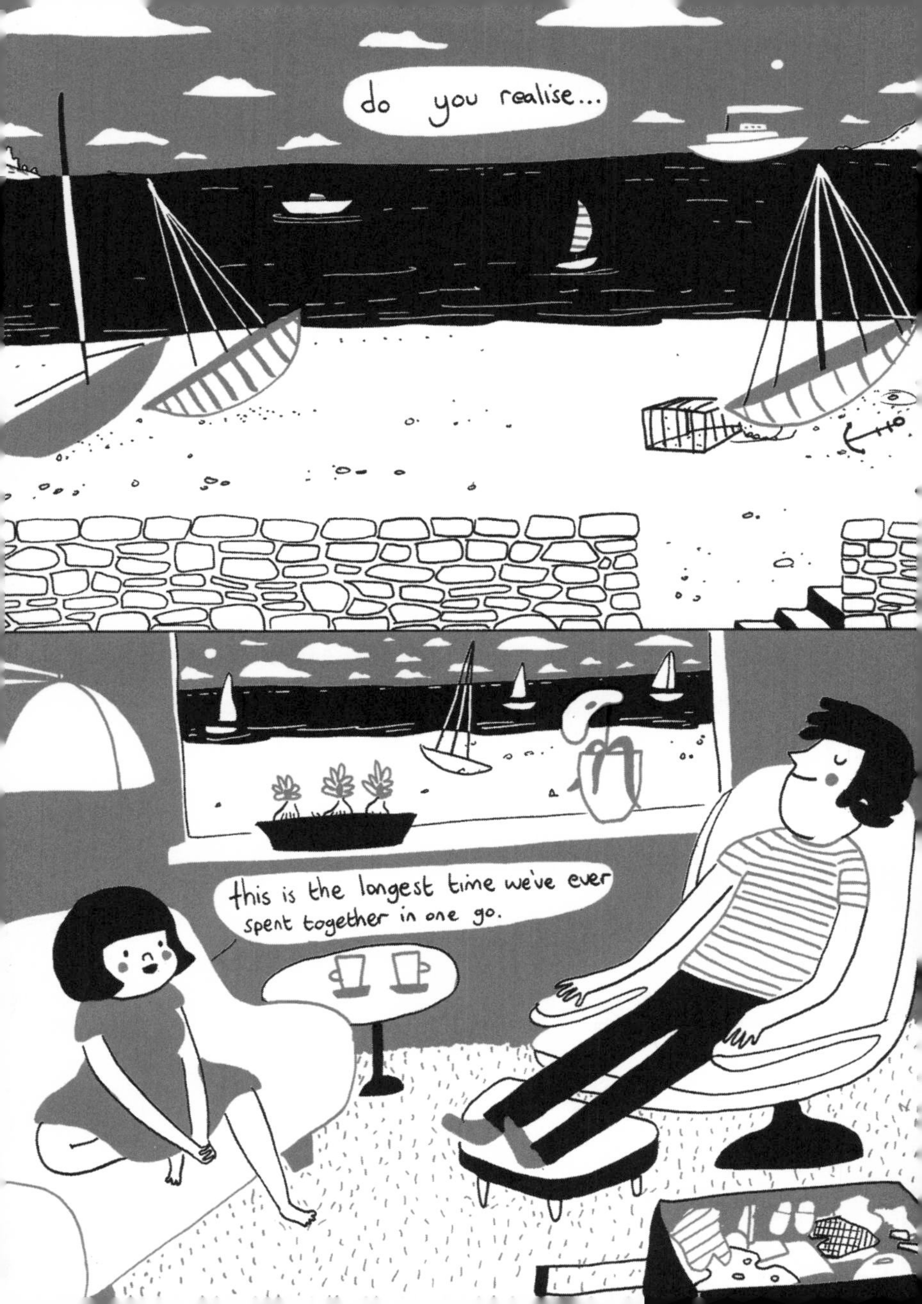
do you realise...
this is the longest time we've ever spent together in one go.

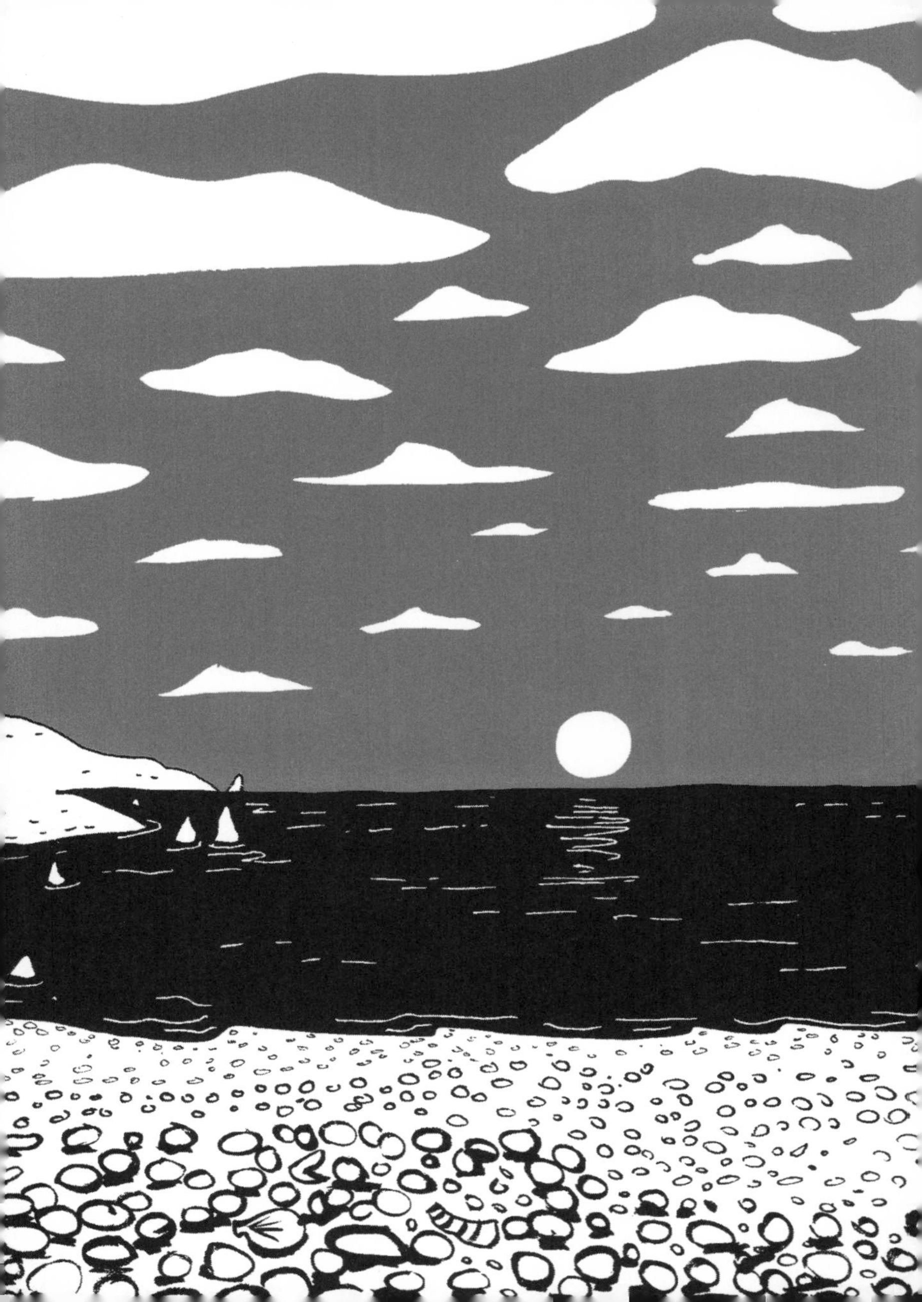

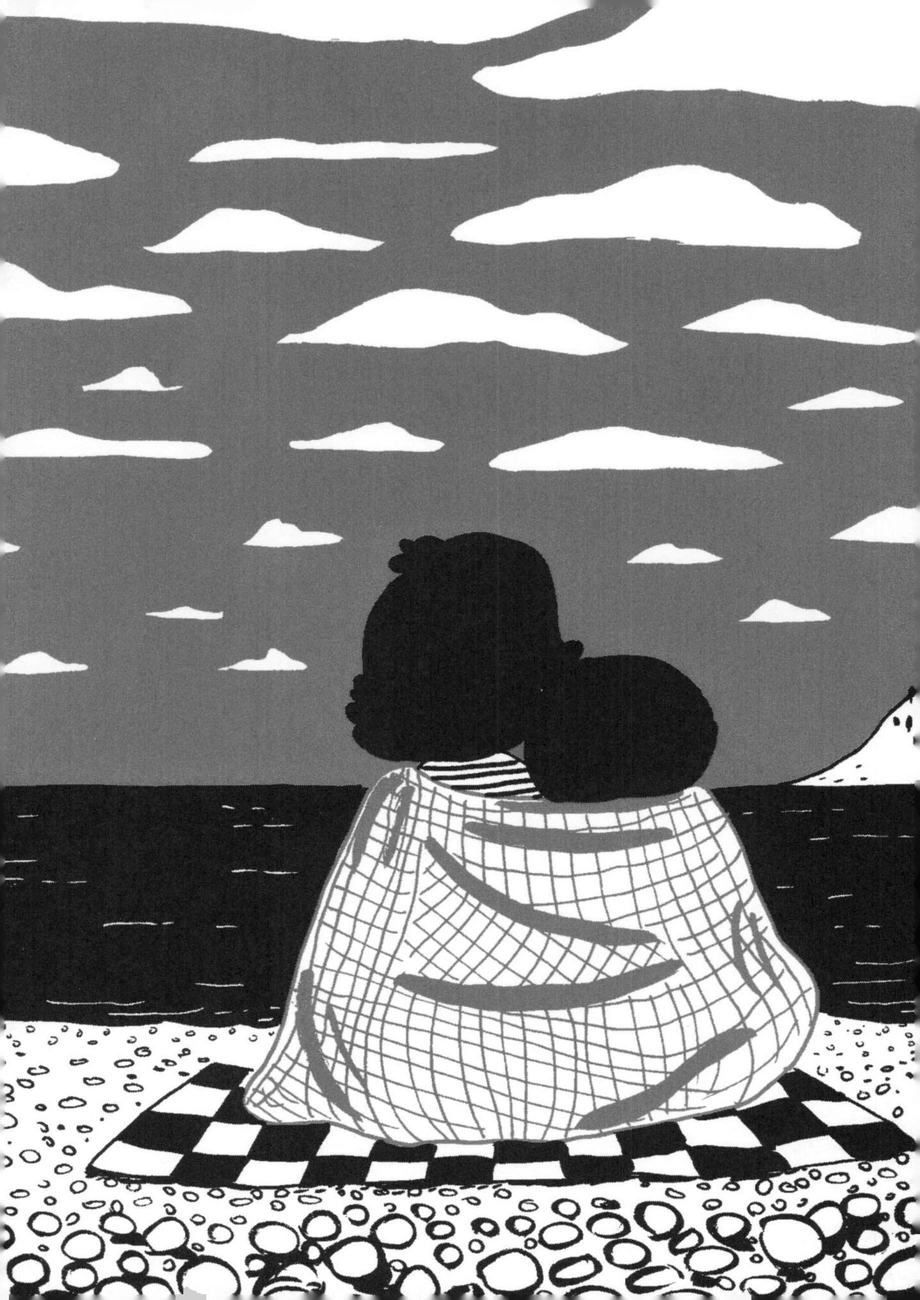

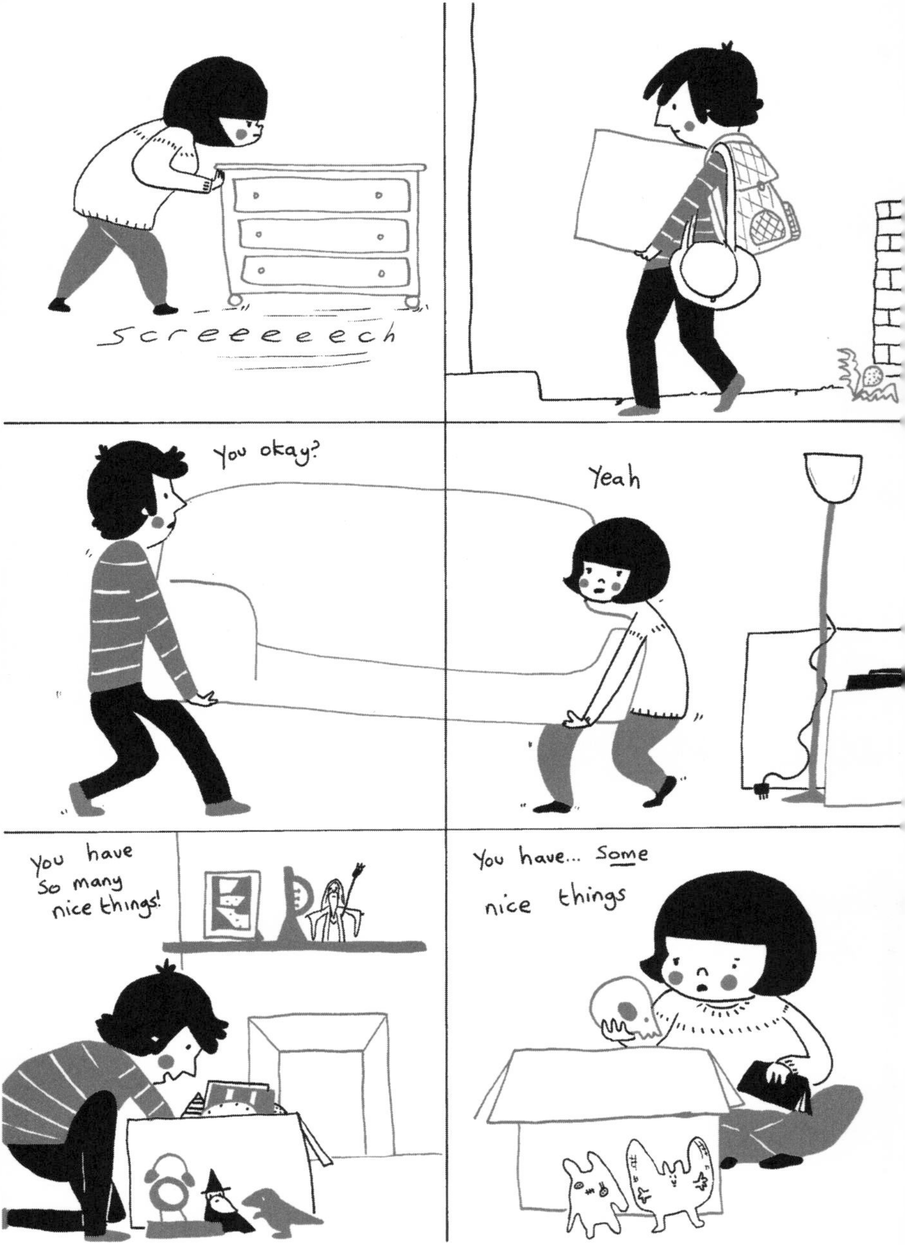
screeeeeech
You okay?
Yeah
You have so many nice things!
You have... some nice things

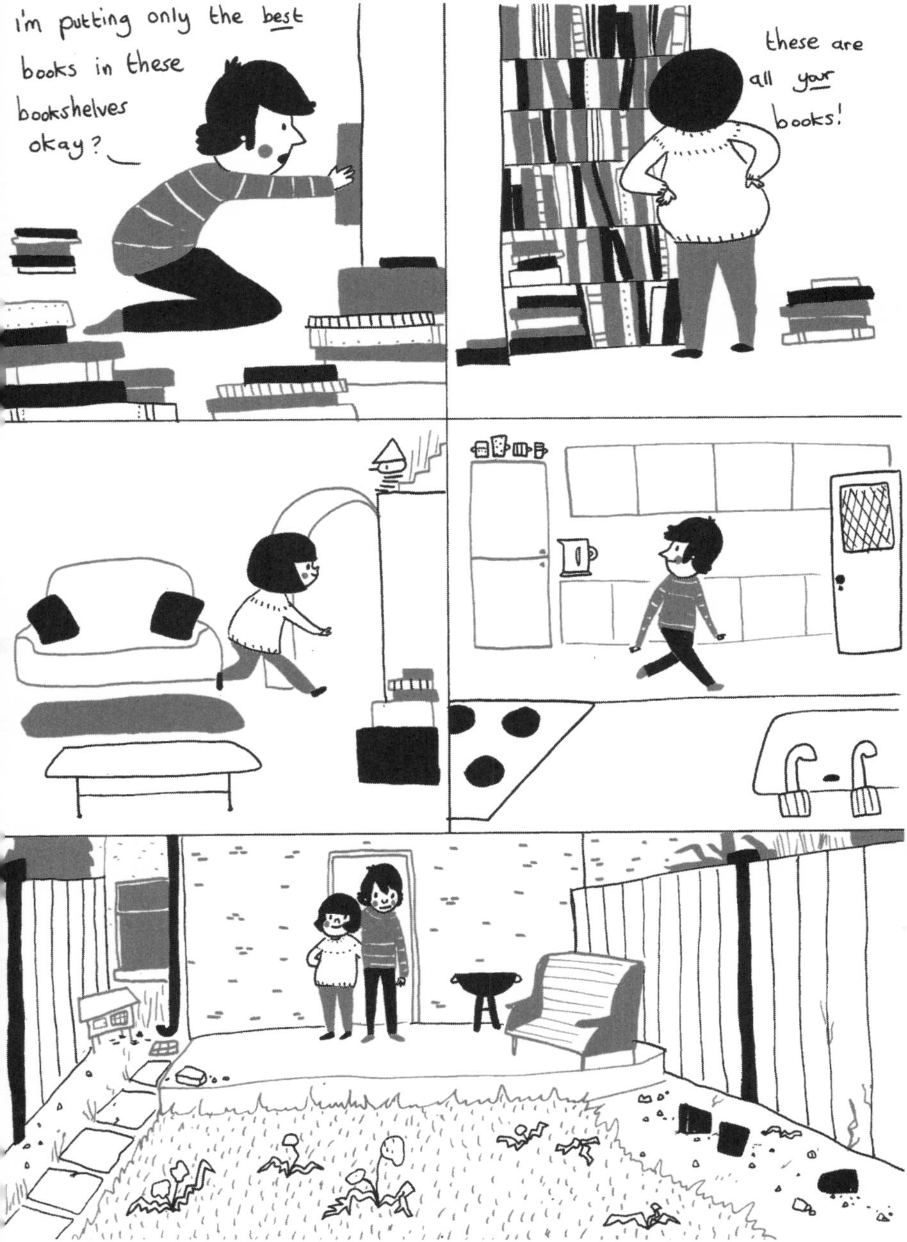
i'm putting only the best books in these bookshelves okay?
these are all your books!

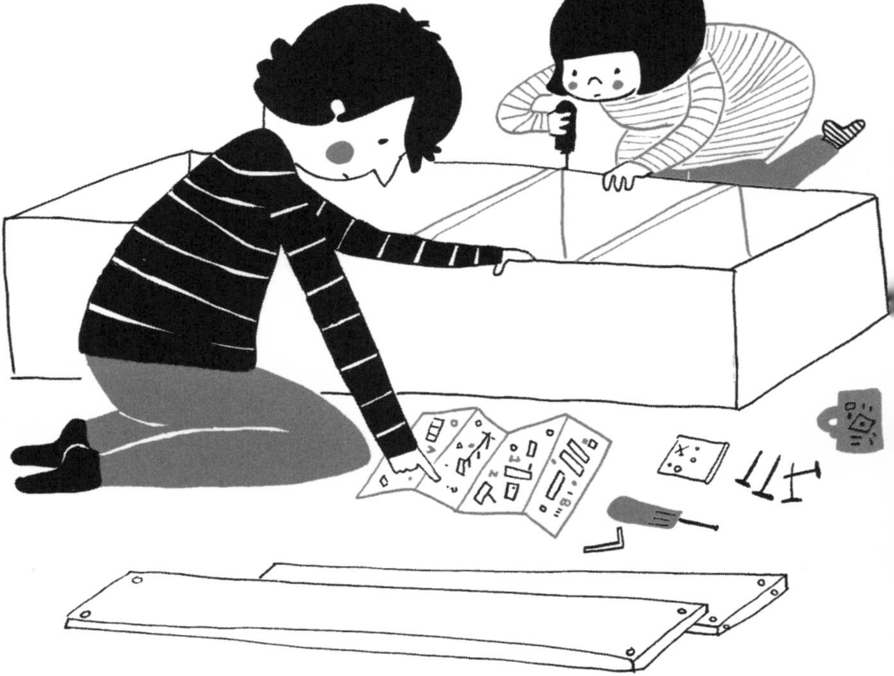

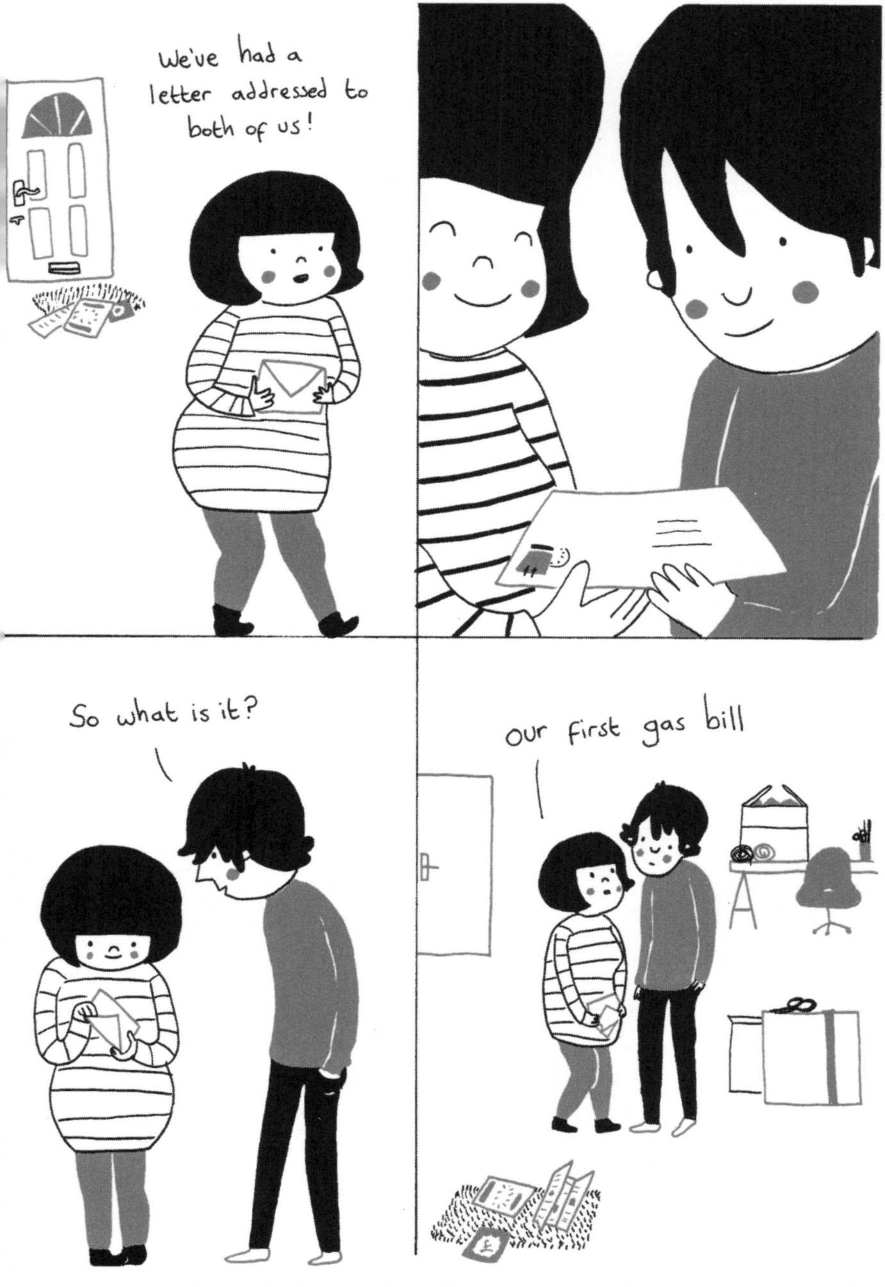
We've had a letter addressed to both of us!
So what is it?
our first gas bill

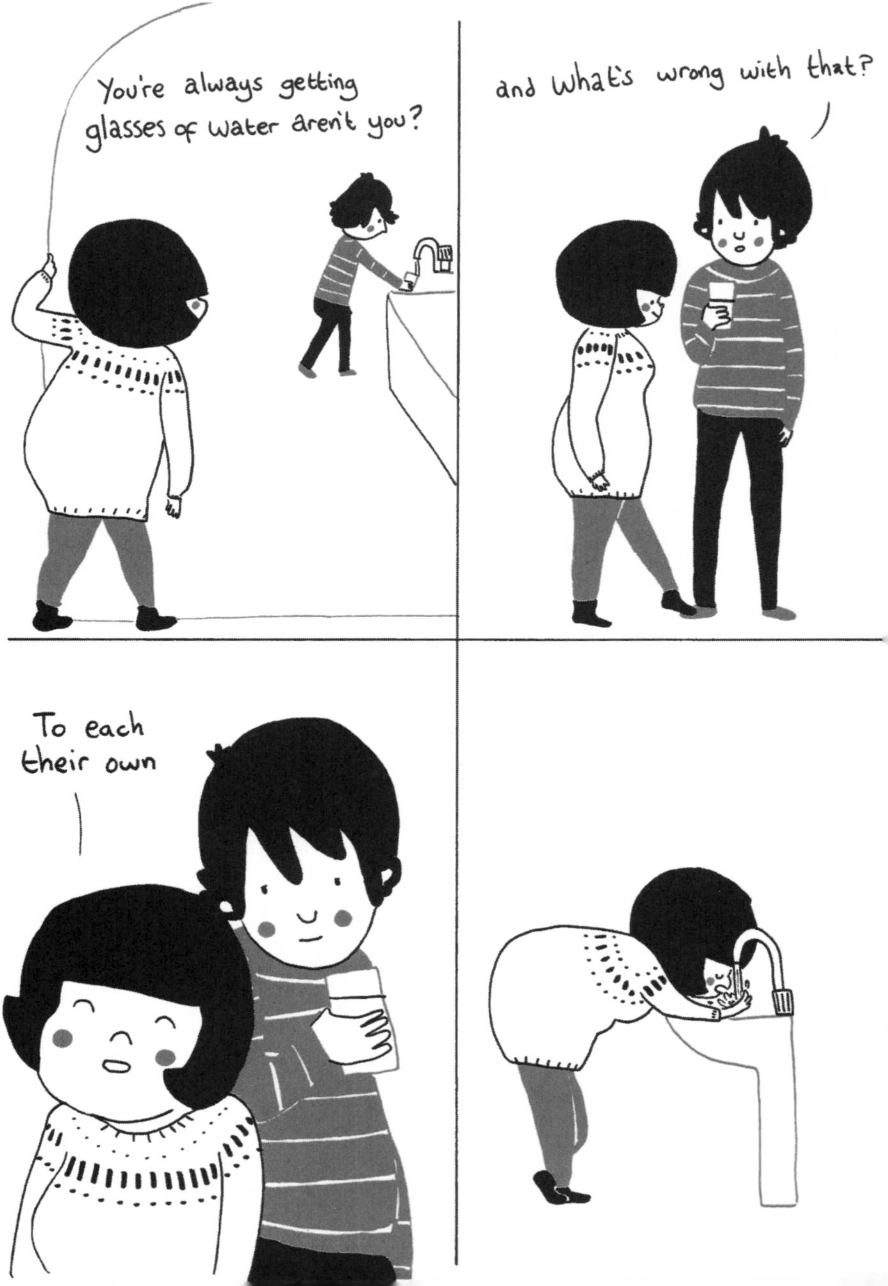
You're always getting glasses of water aren't you?
and what's wrong with that?
To each their own

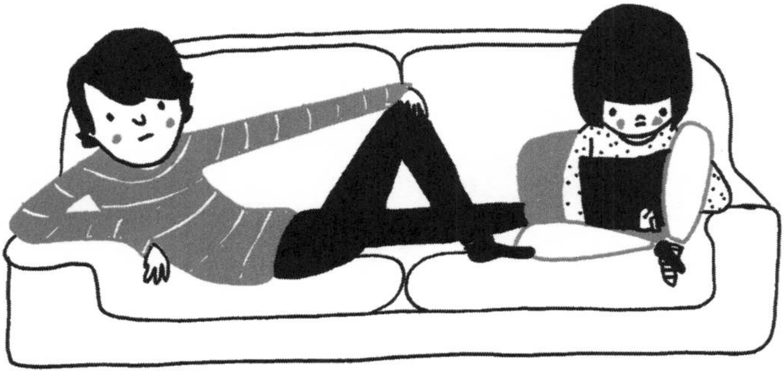

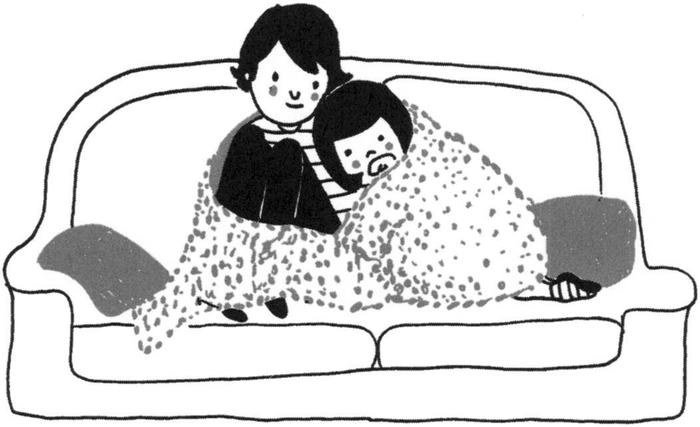

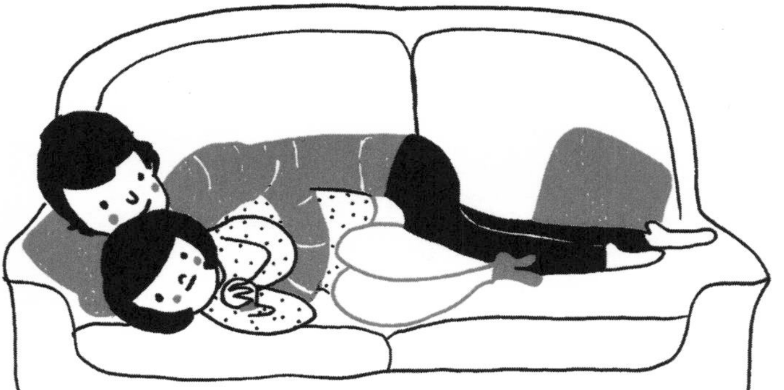

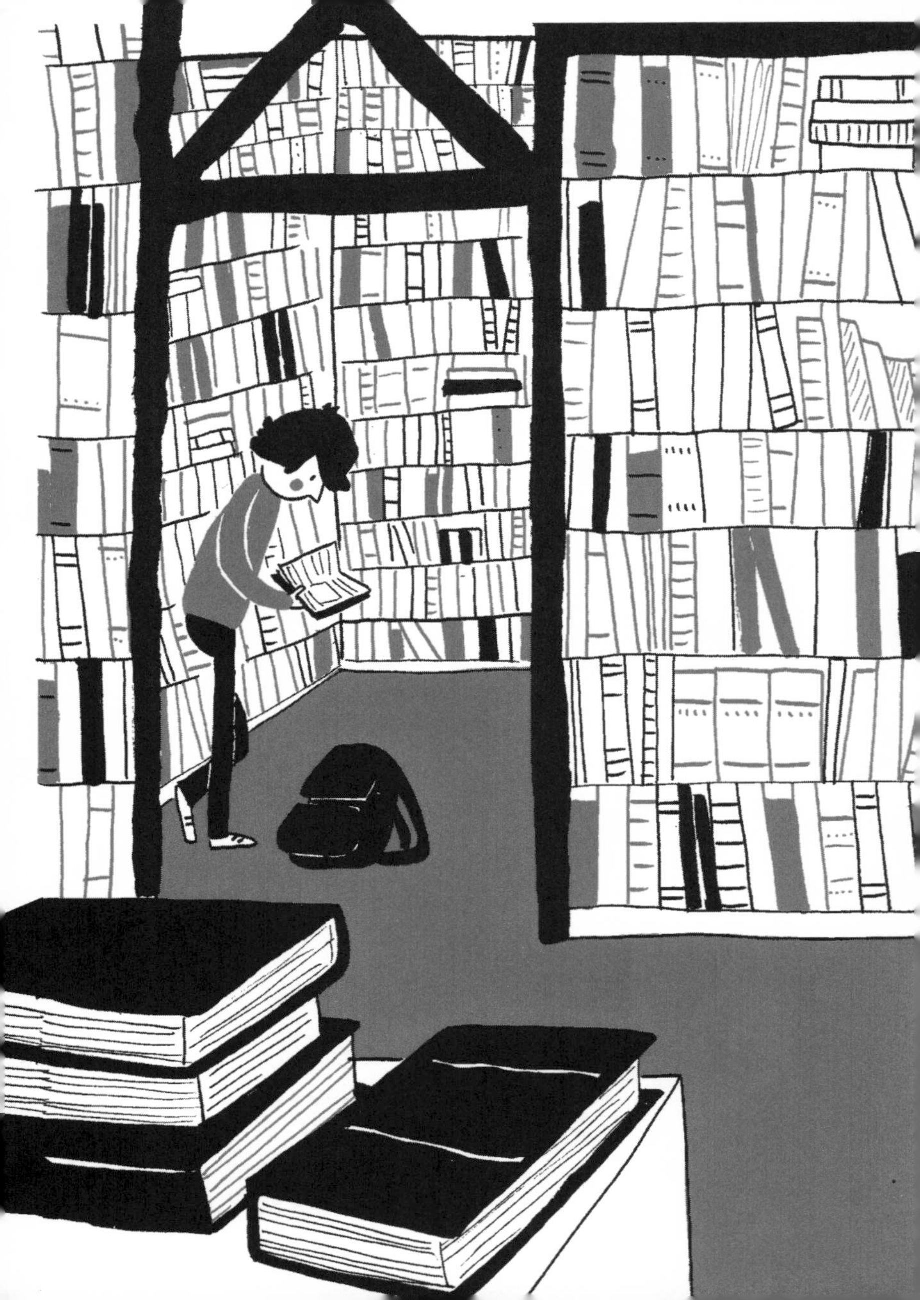

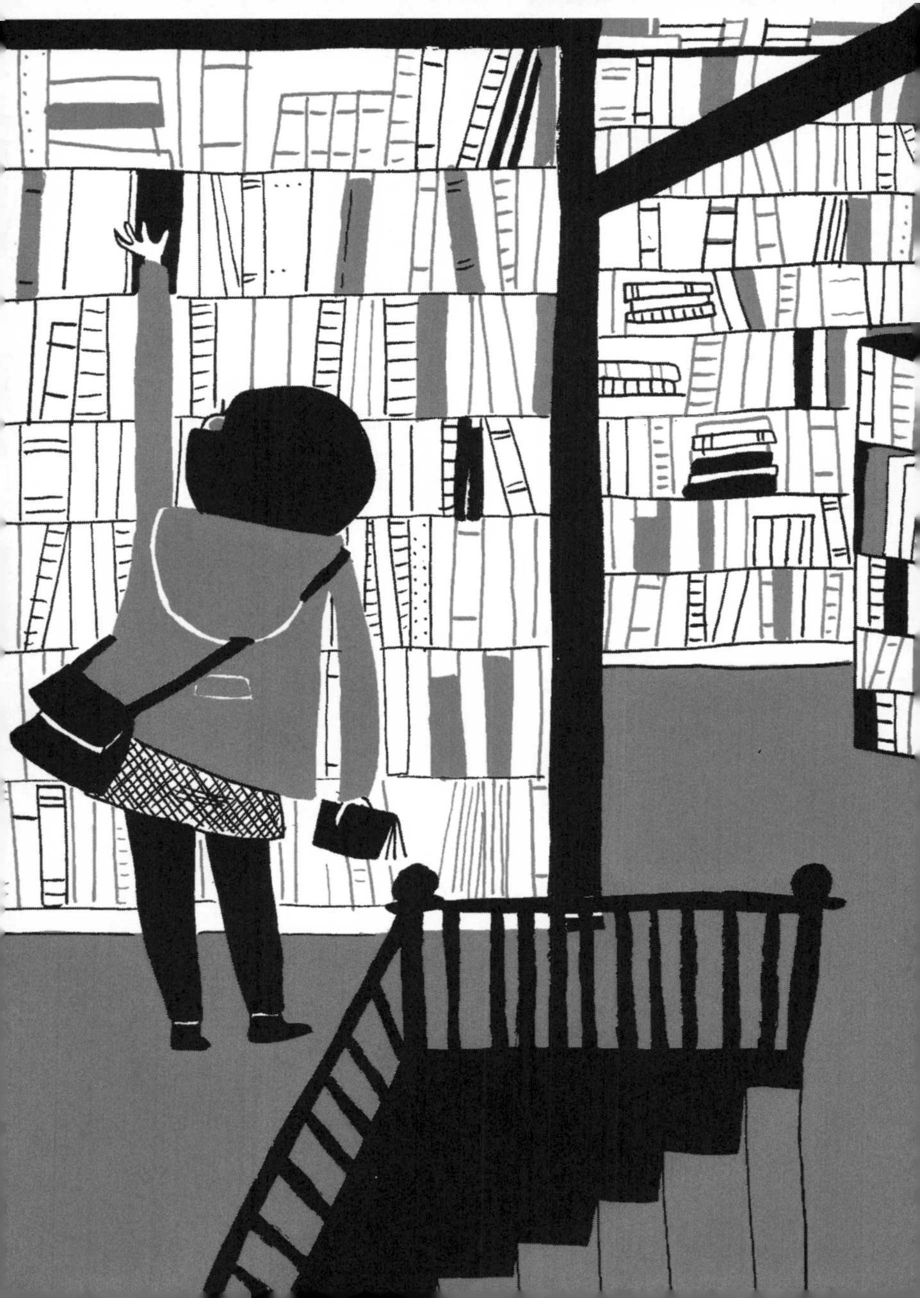

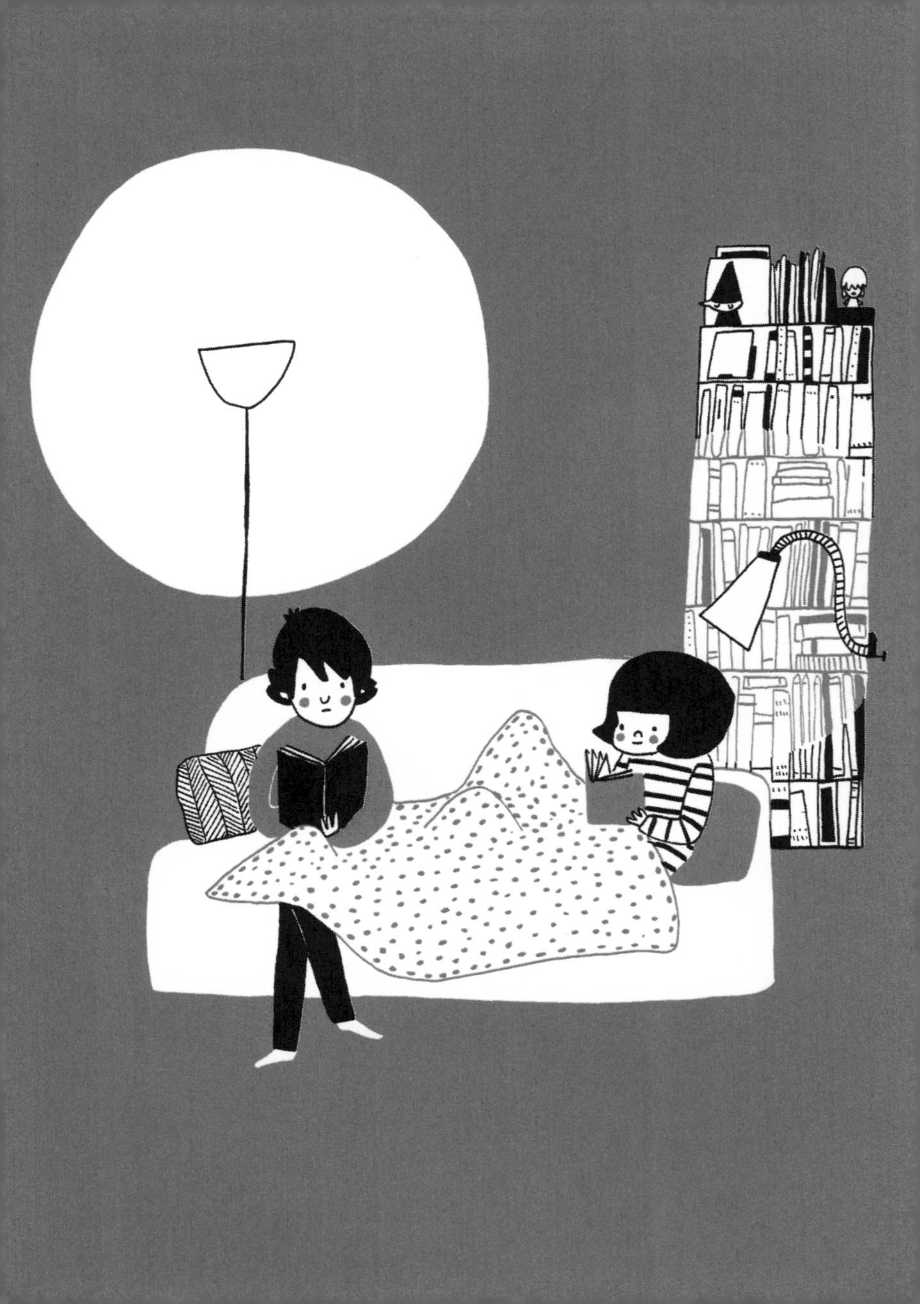

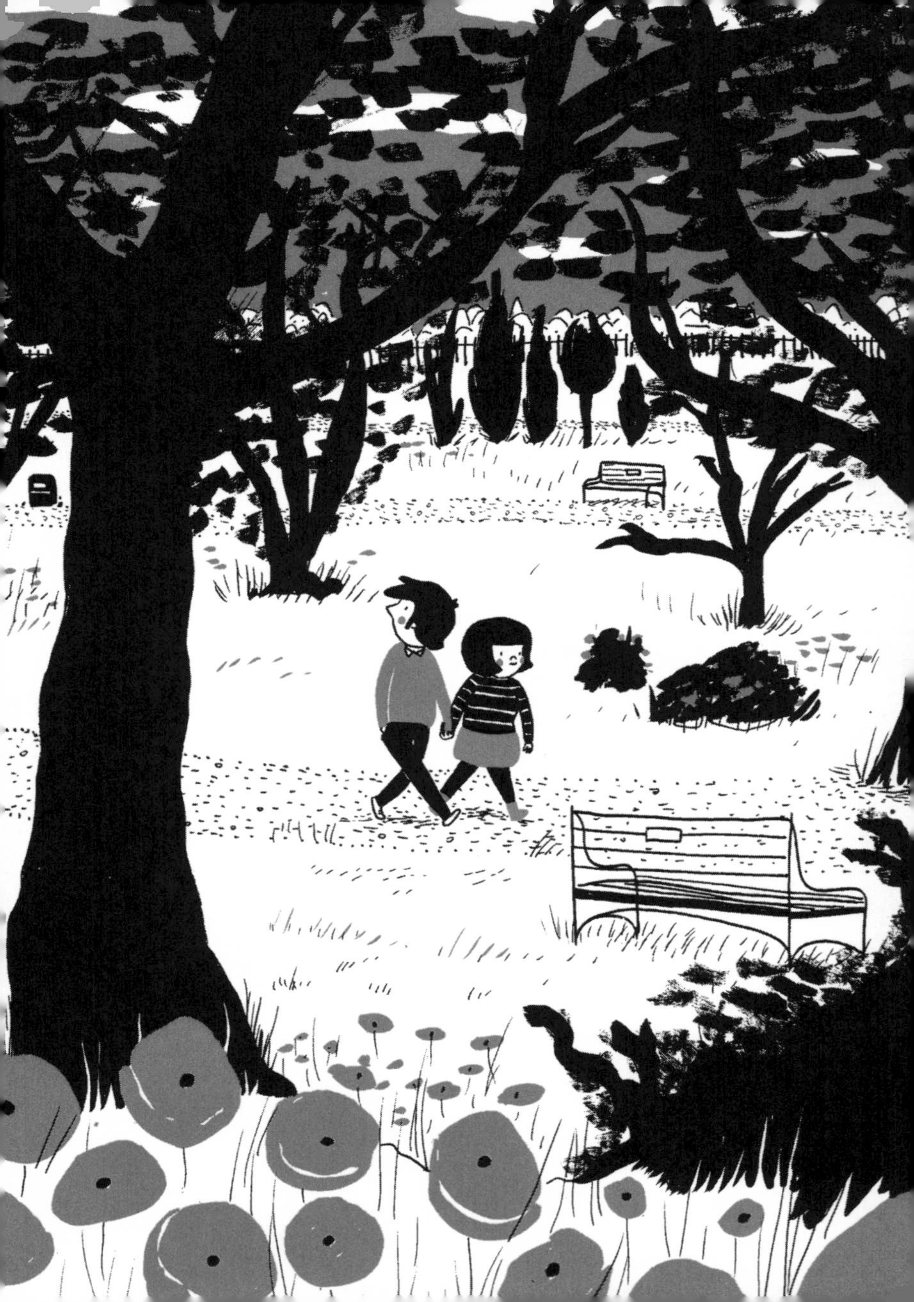

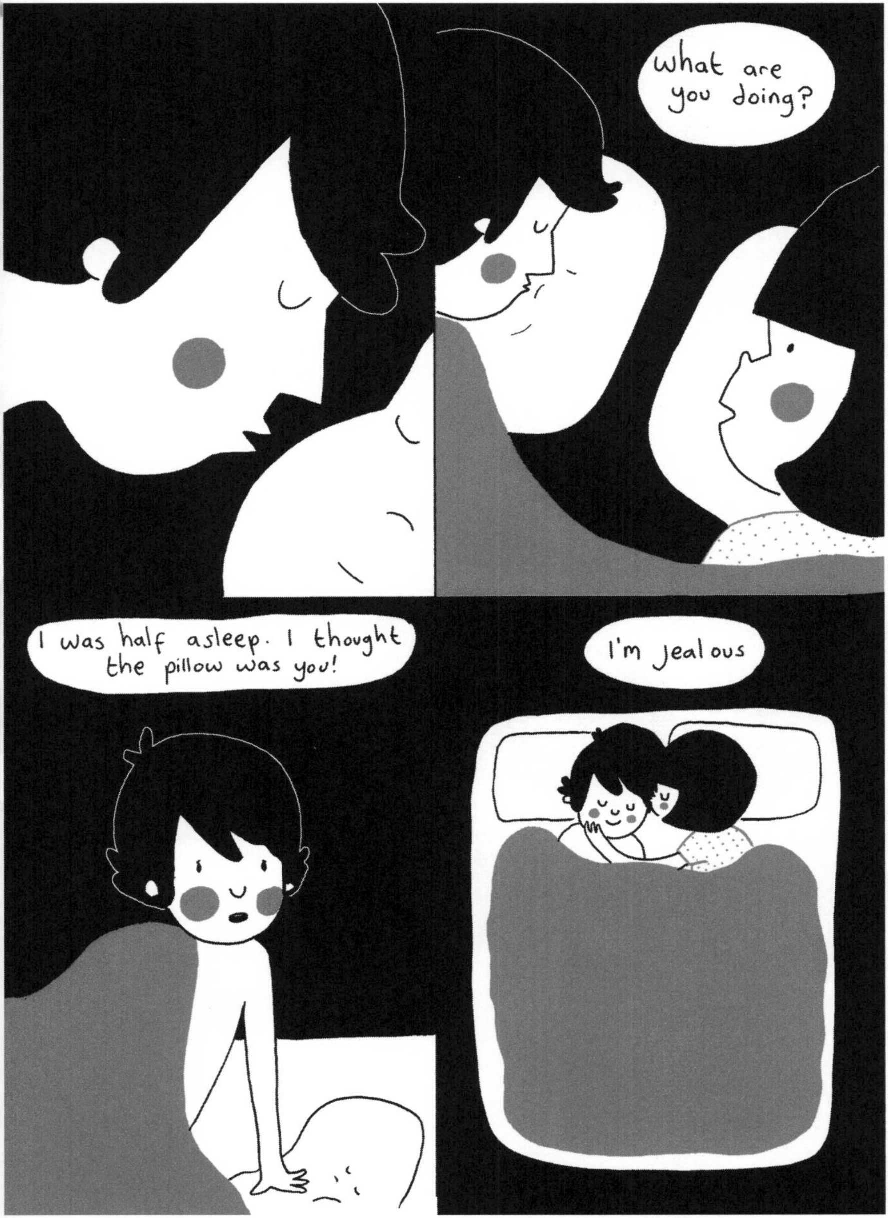
what are you doing?
I was half asleep. I thought the pillow was you!
I'm jealous

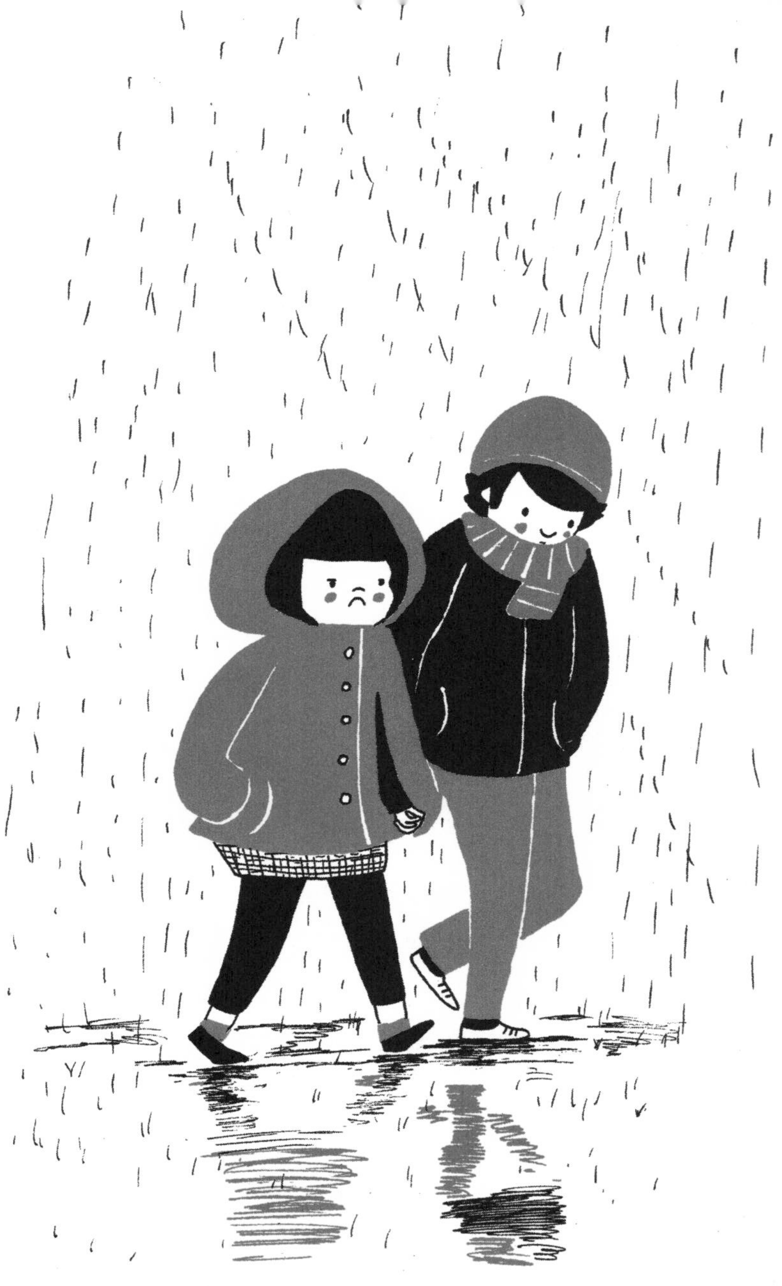

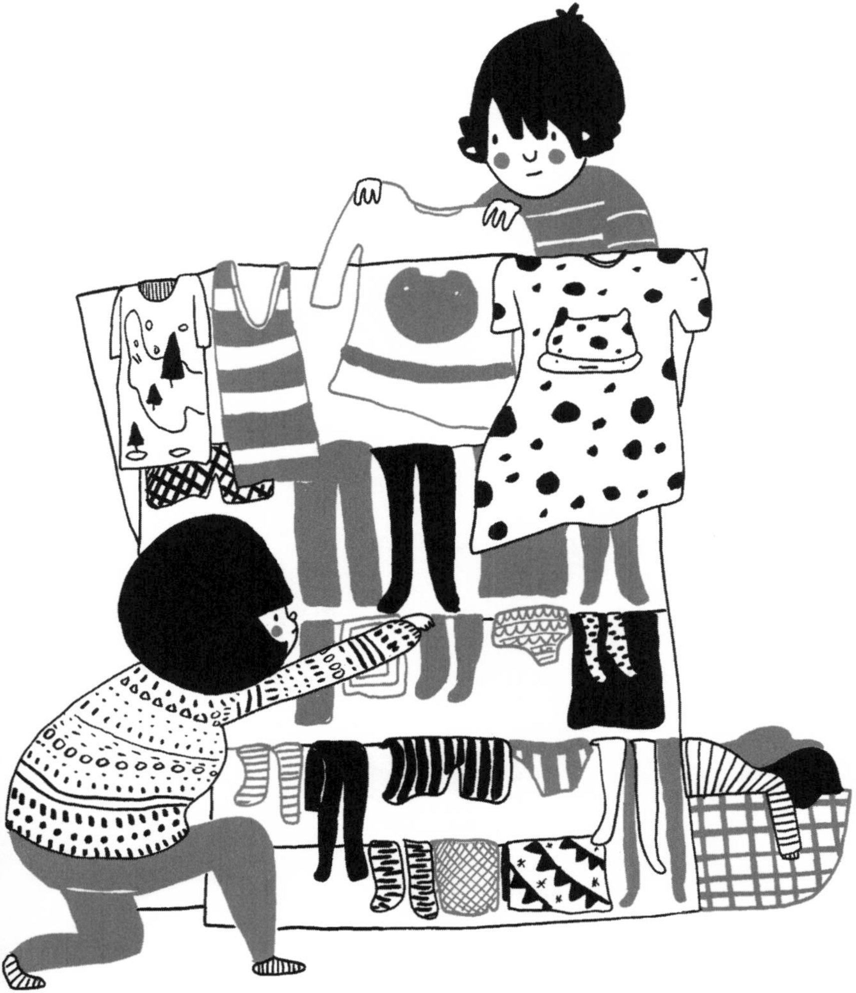

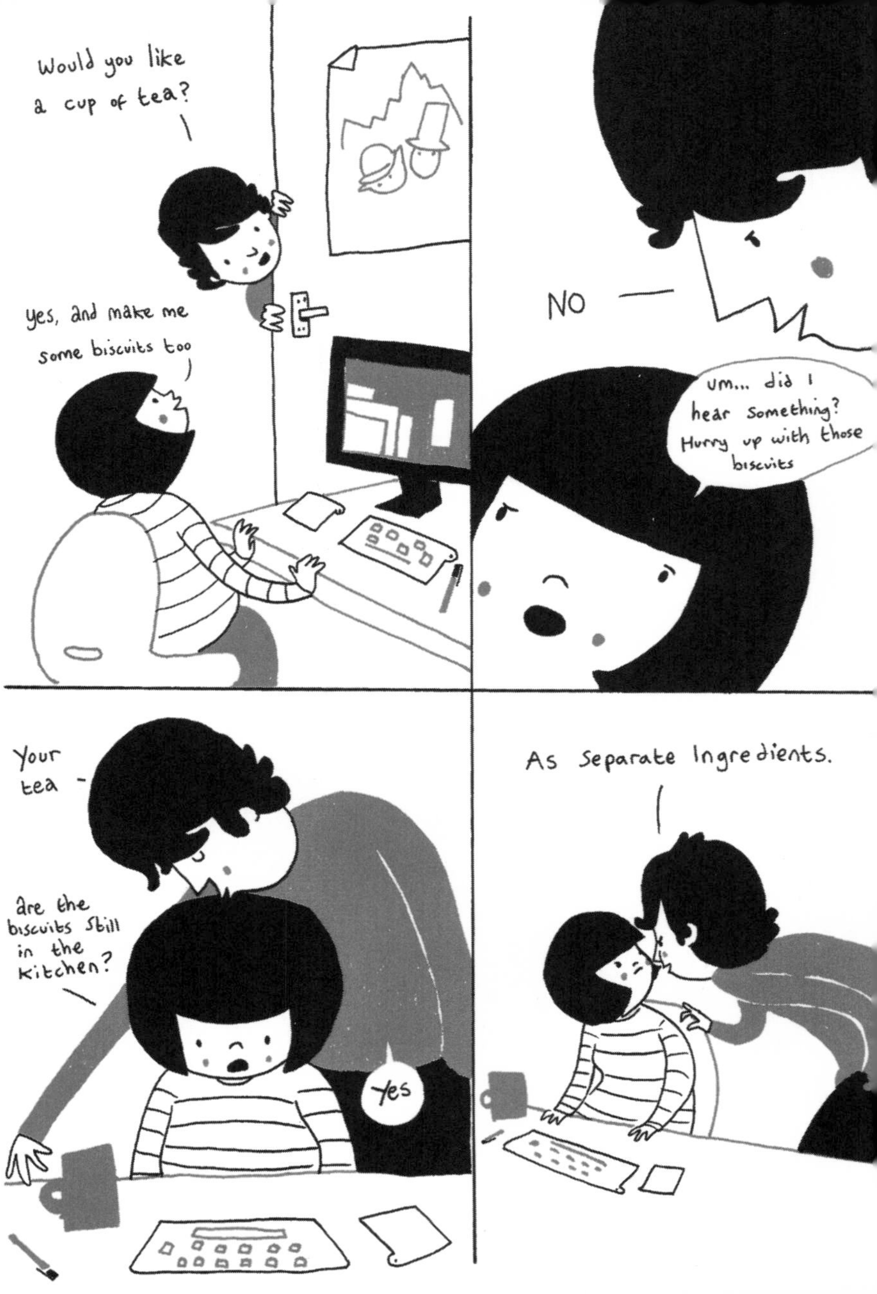
Would you like a cup of tea?
yes, and make me some biscuits too
NO
um... did I hear something? Hurry up with those biscuits
Your tea
are the biscuits still in the kitchen?
Yes
As Separate Ingredients.

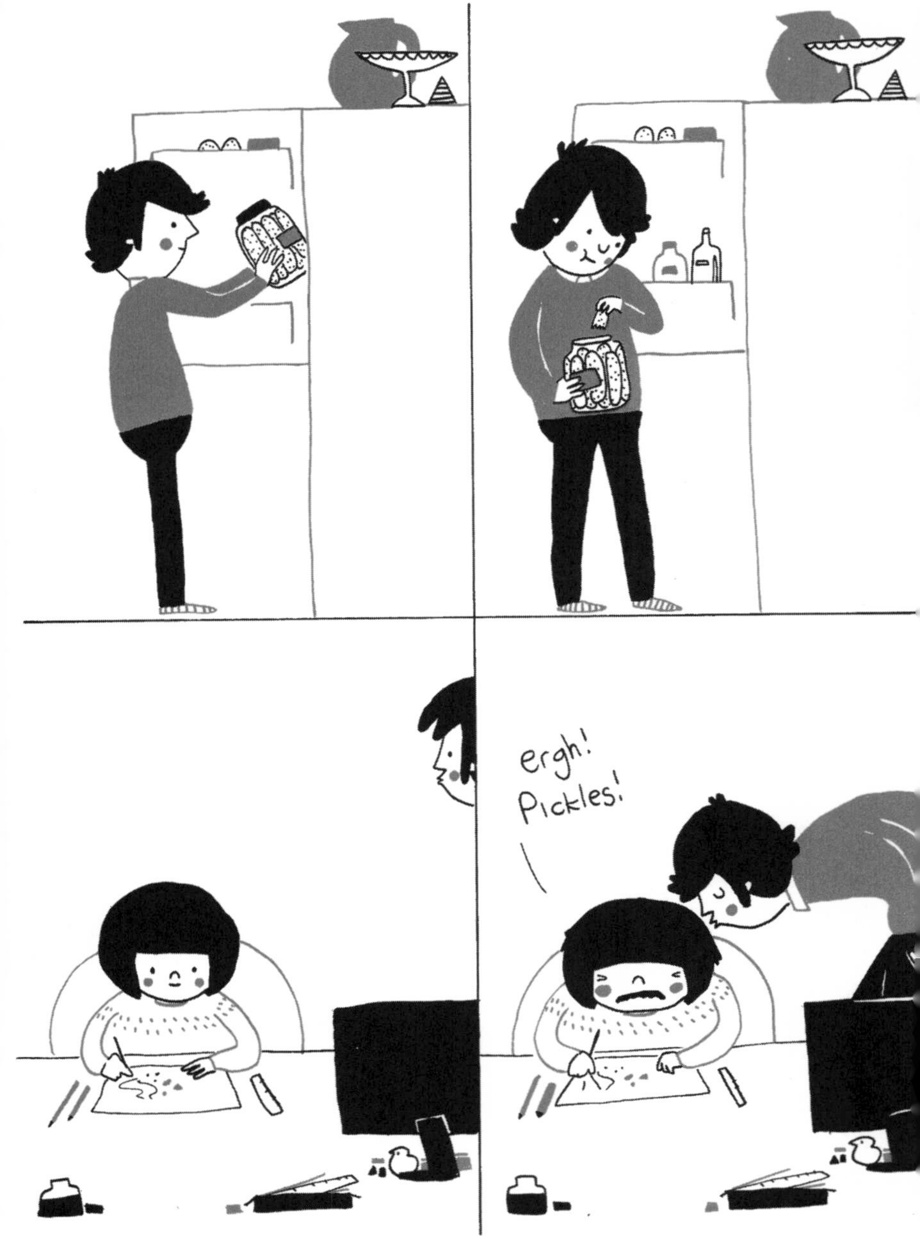
ergh! Pickles!

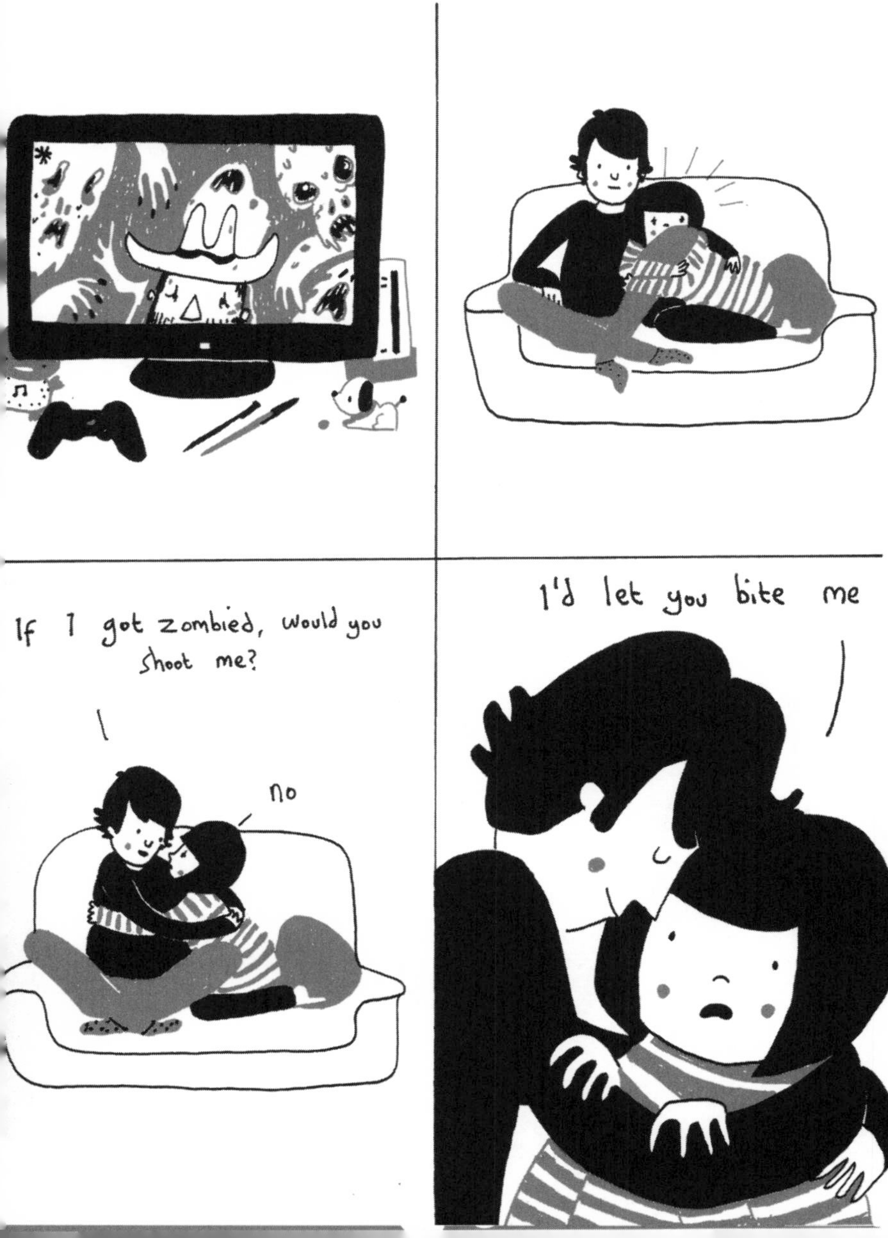
If I got zombied, would you shoot me?
no
I'd let you bite me

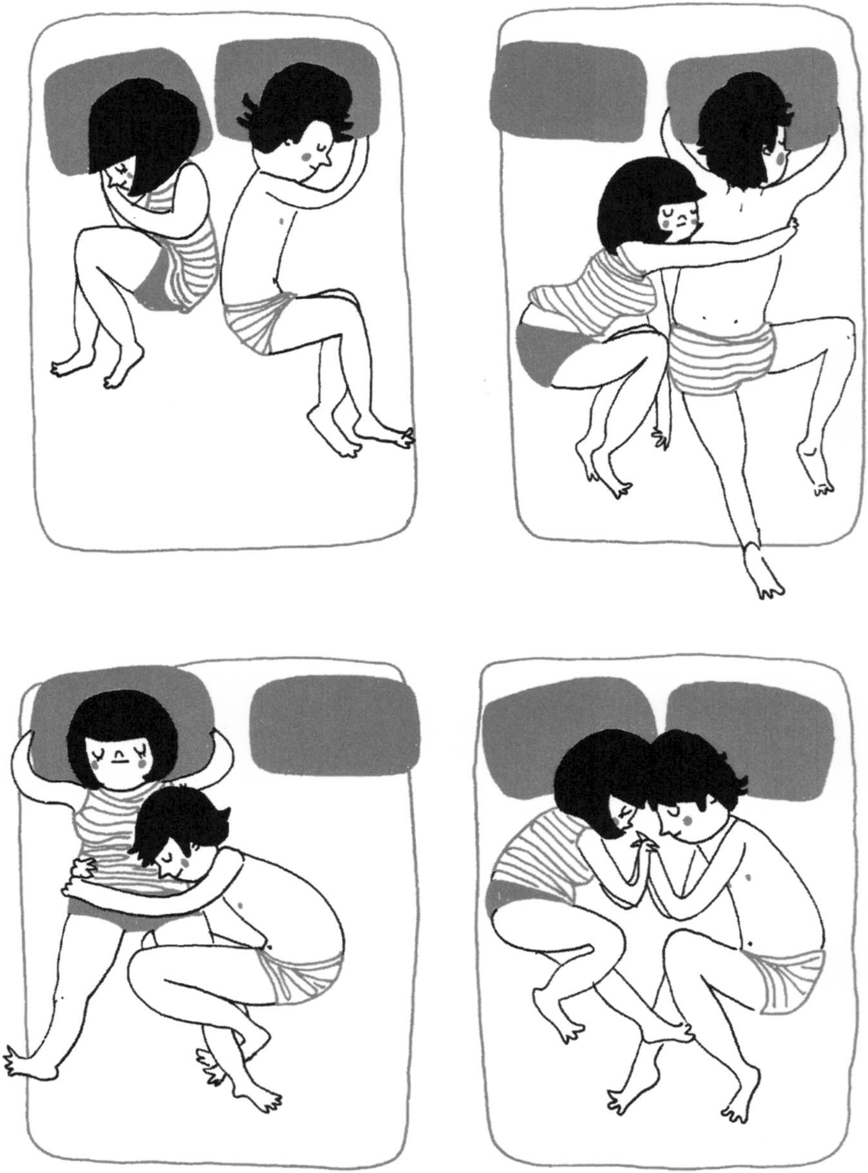

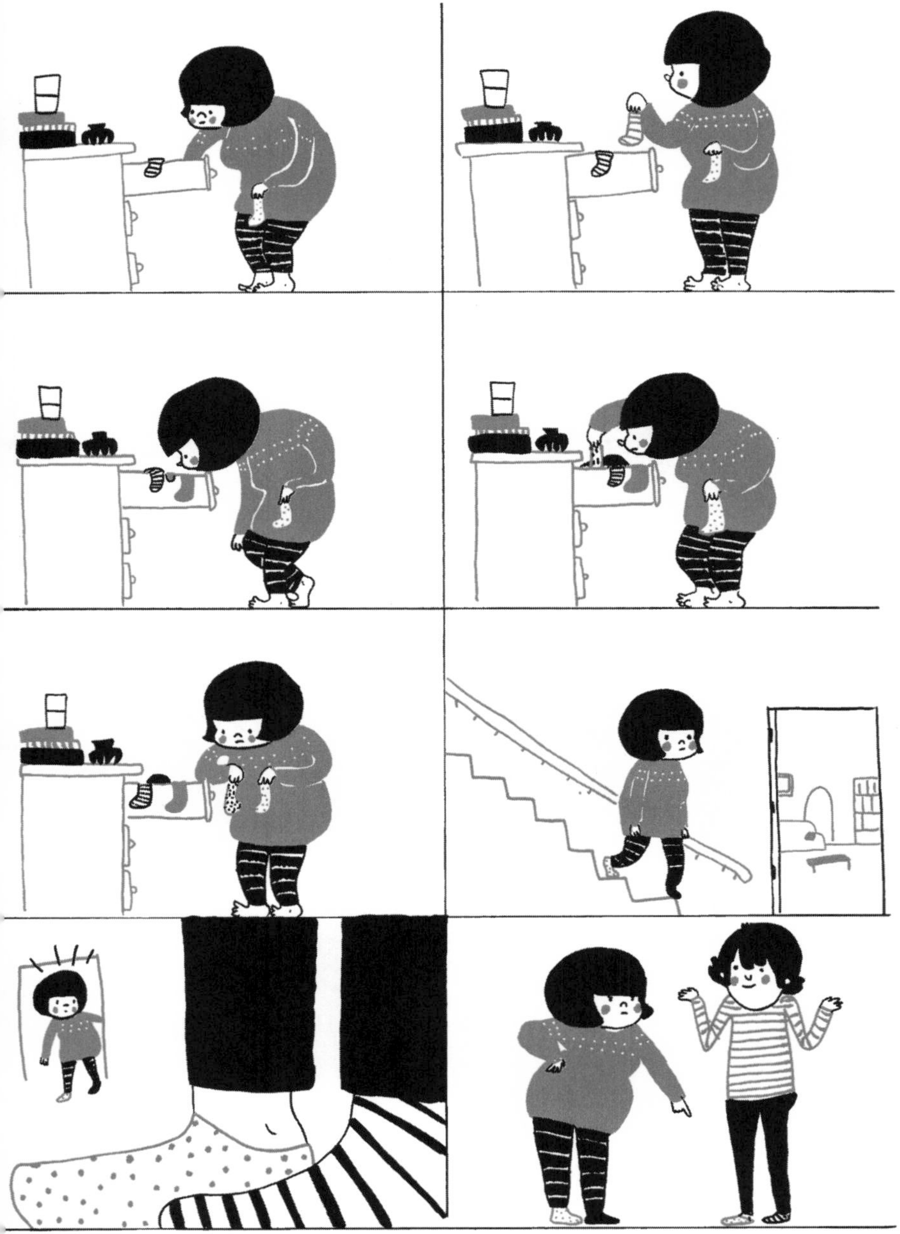

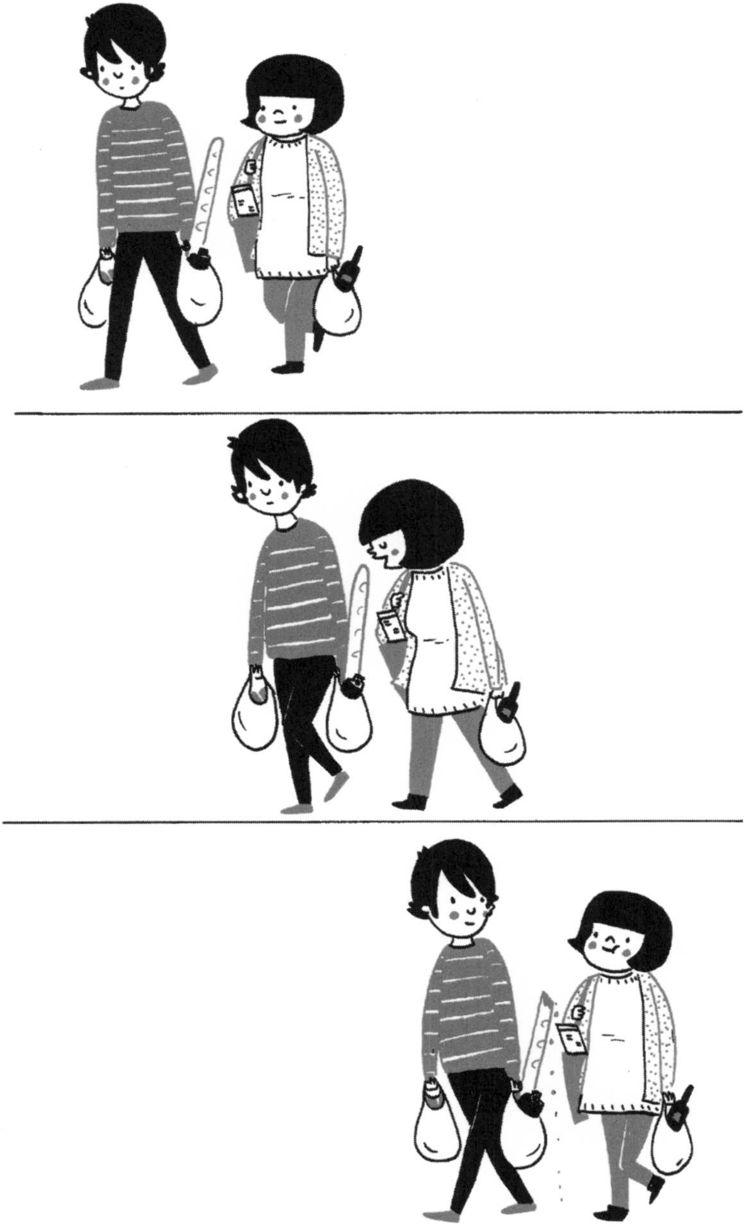

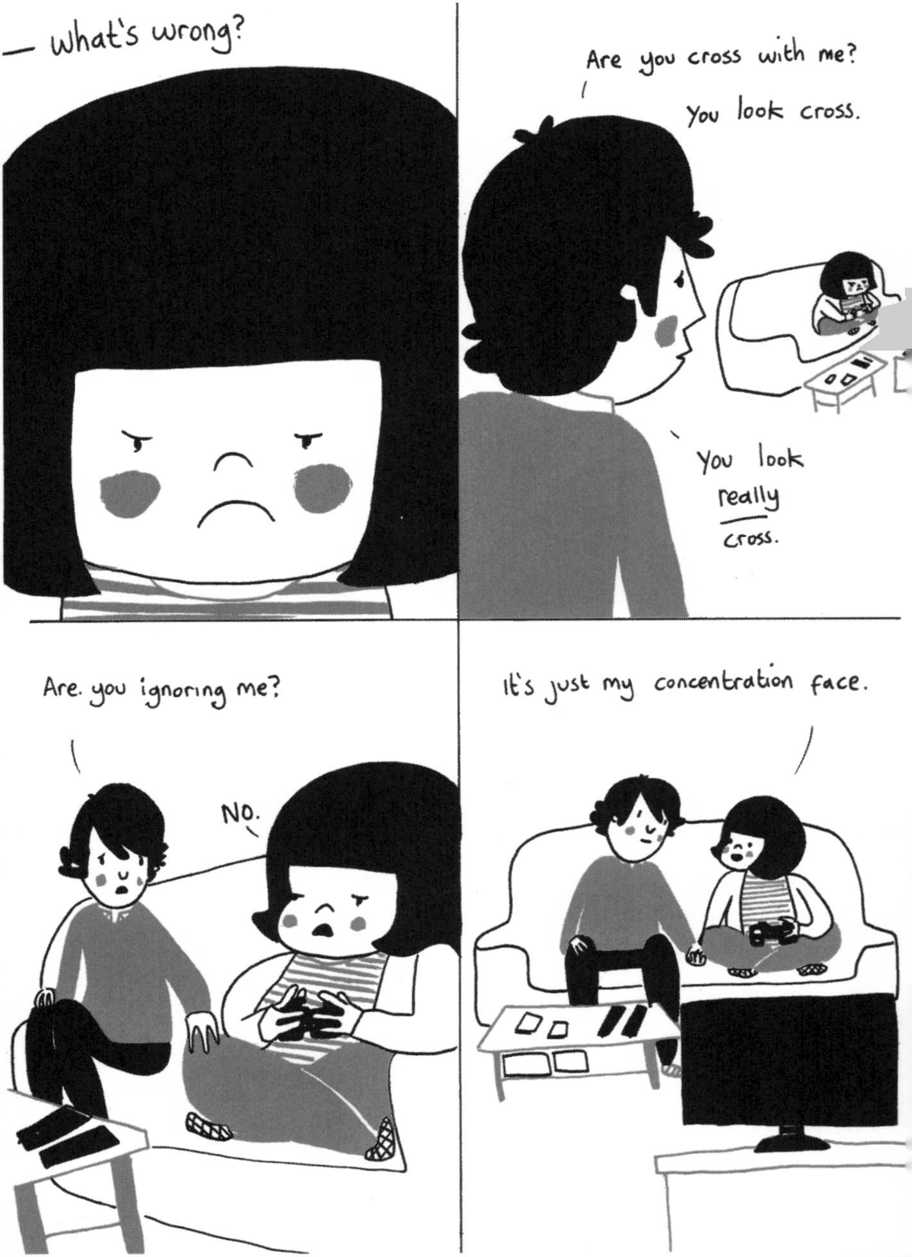

— what's wrong?
Are you cross with me?
You look cross.
You look really cross.
Are. you ignoring me?
No.
It's just my concentration face.

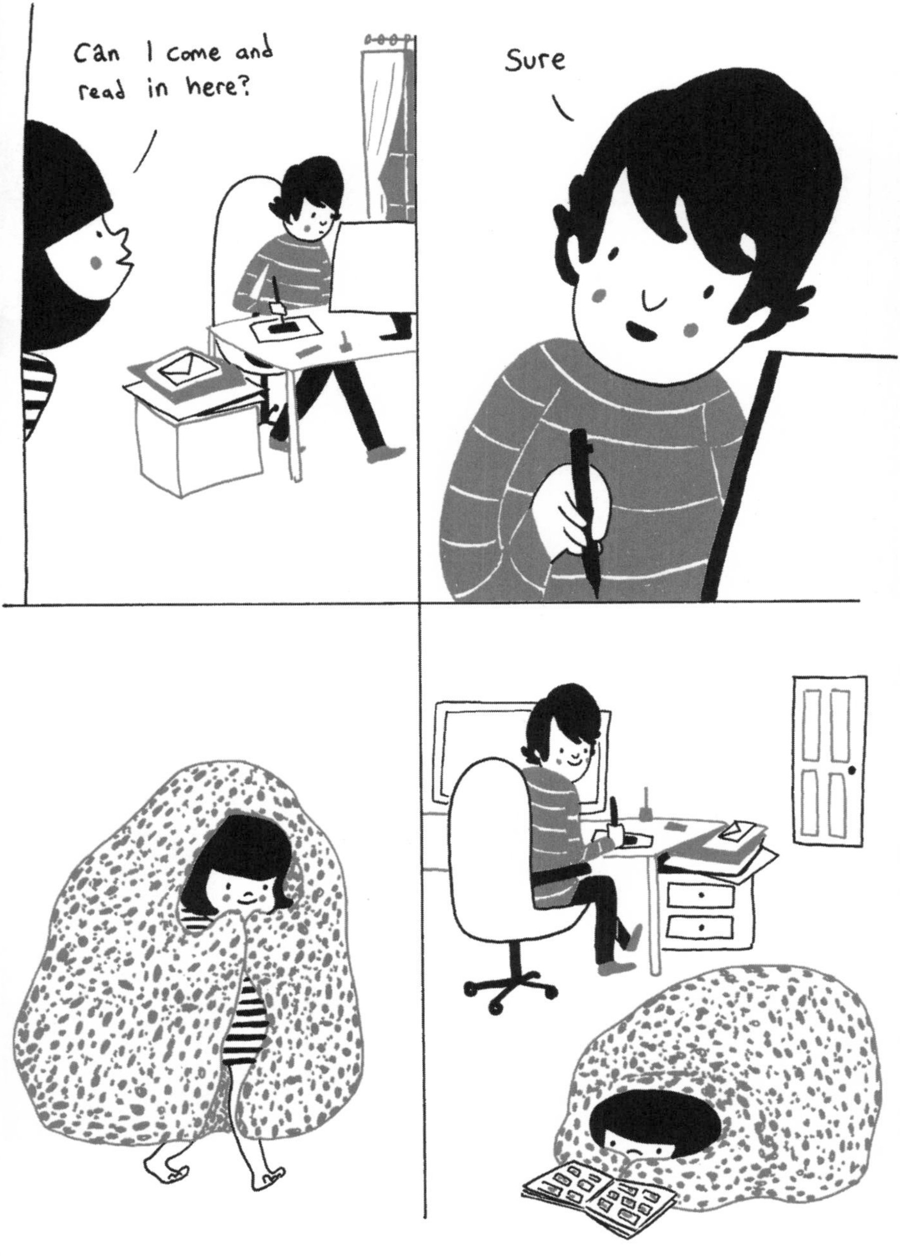
Can I come and read in here?
Sure

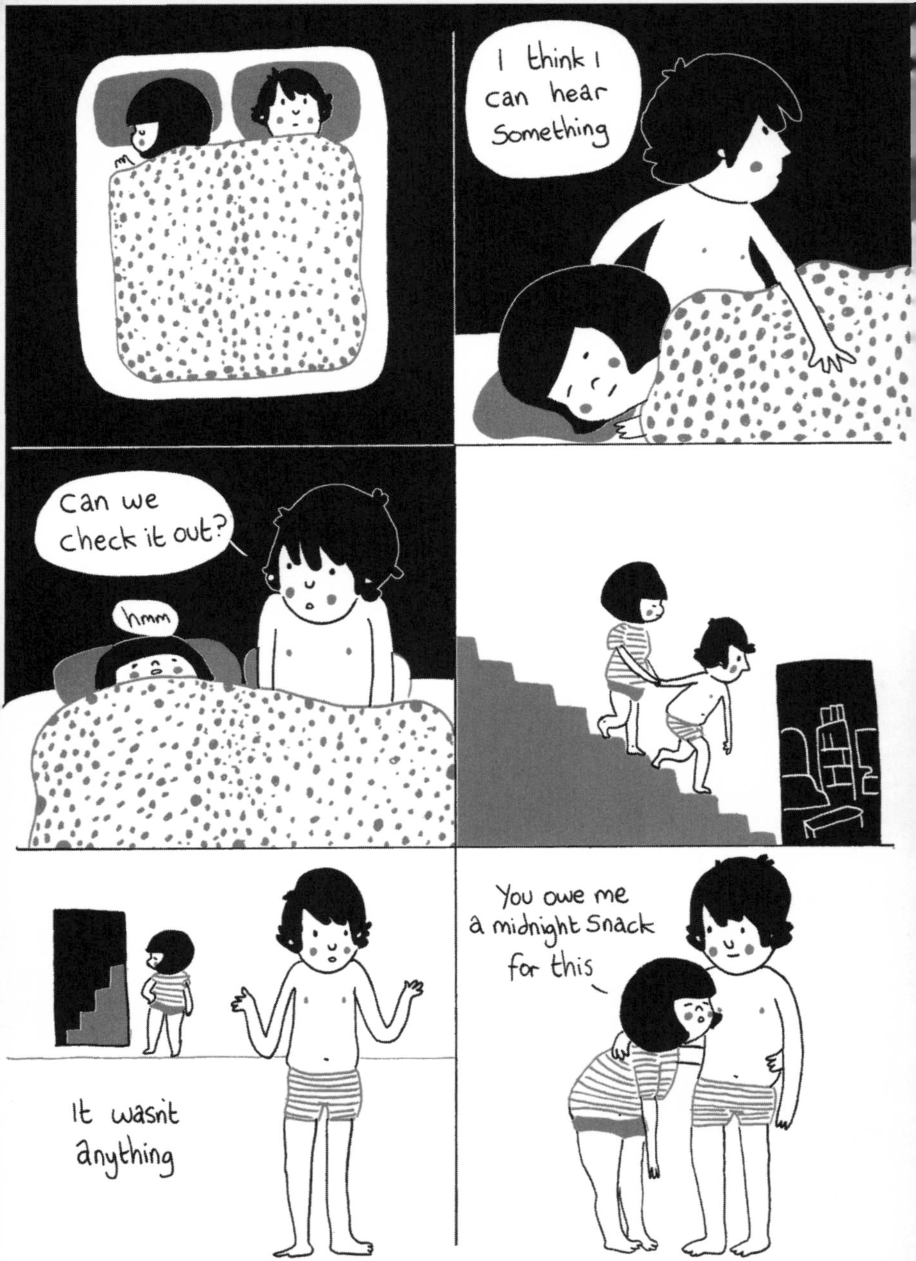
m
I think I can hear Something
Can we check it out?
hmm
It wasnt anything
You owe me a midnight Snack for this

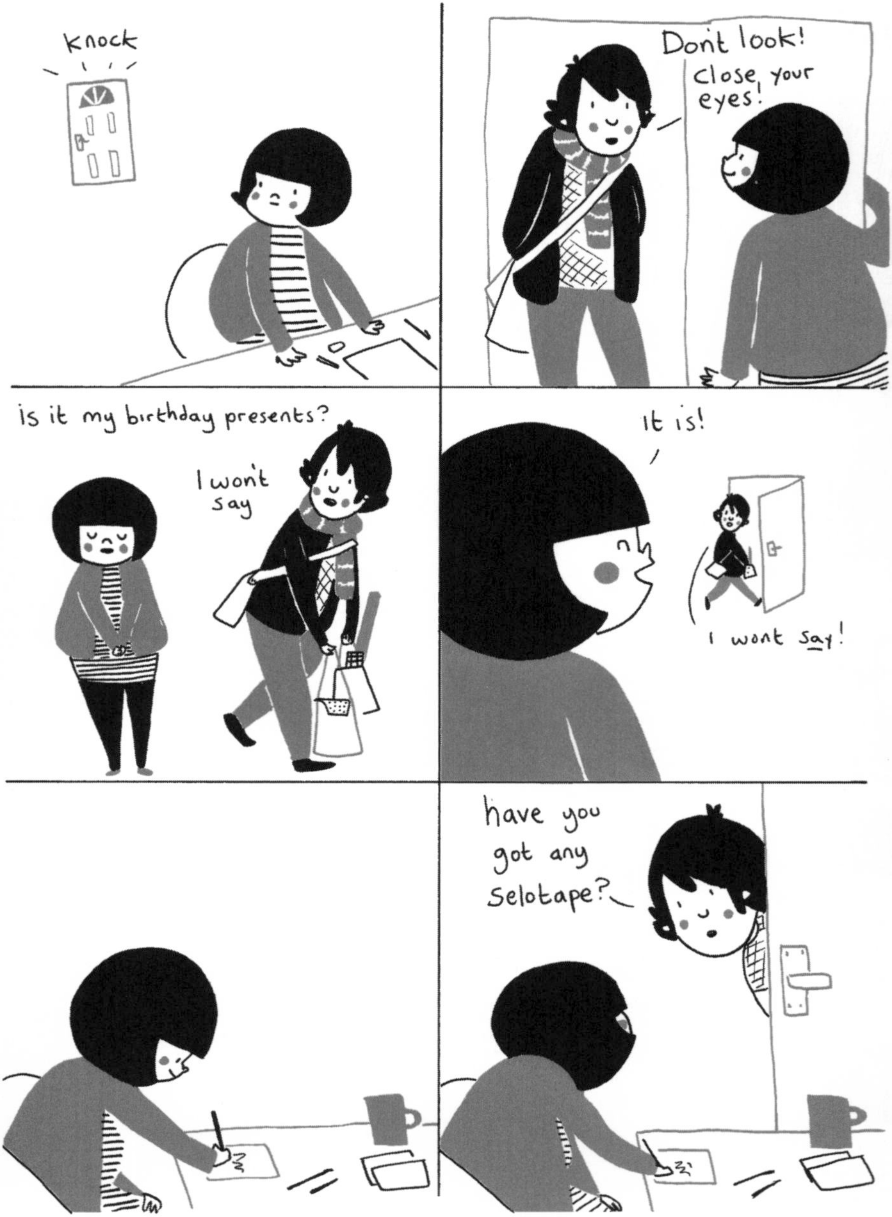
knock
Don't look! Close your eyes!
is it my birthday presents?
I won't say
It is!
I wont say!
have you got any Selotape?

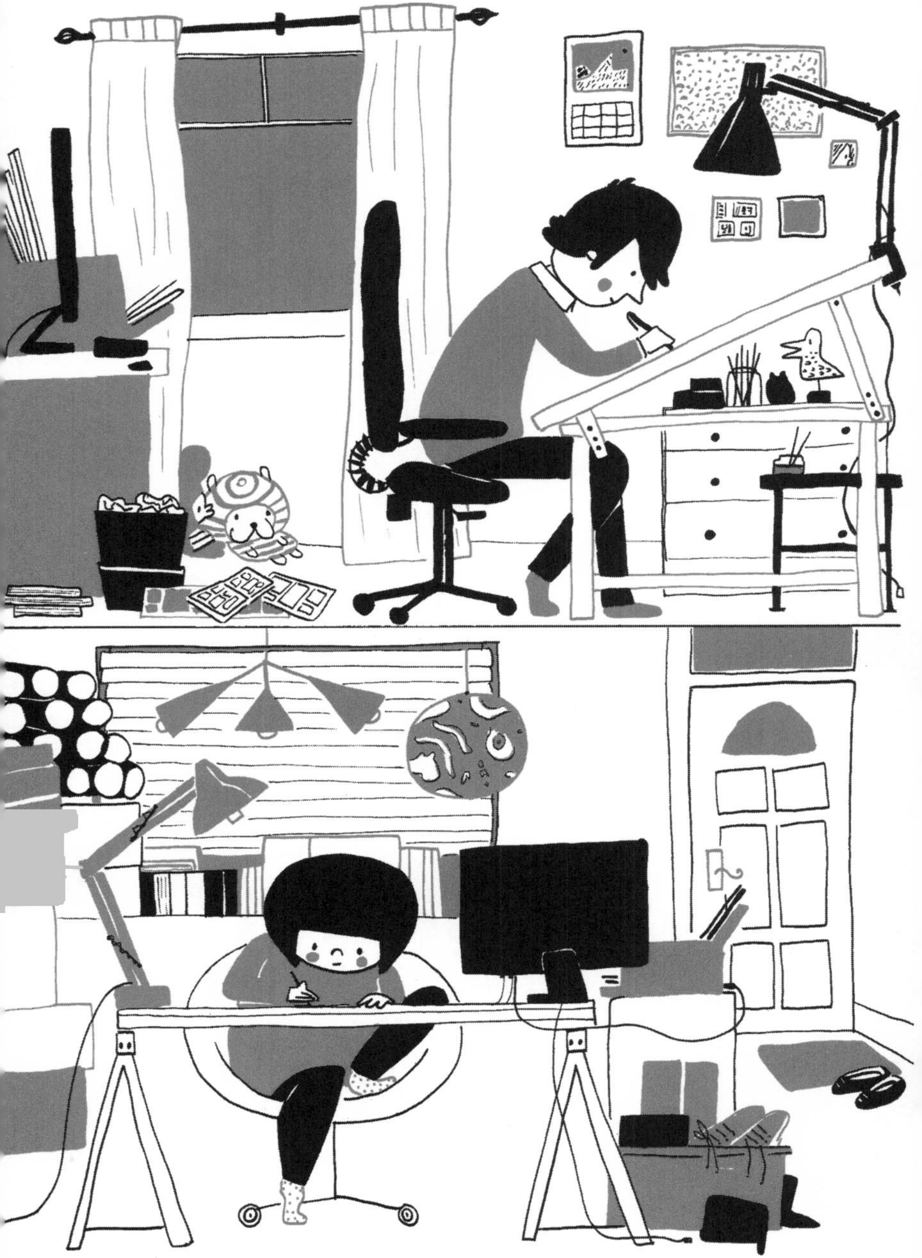

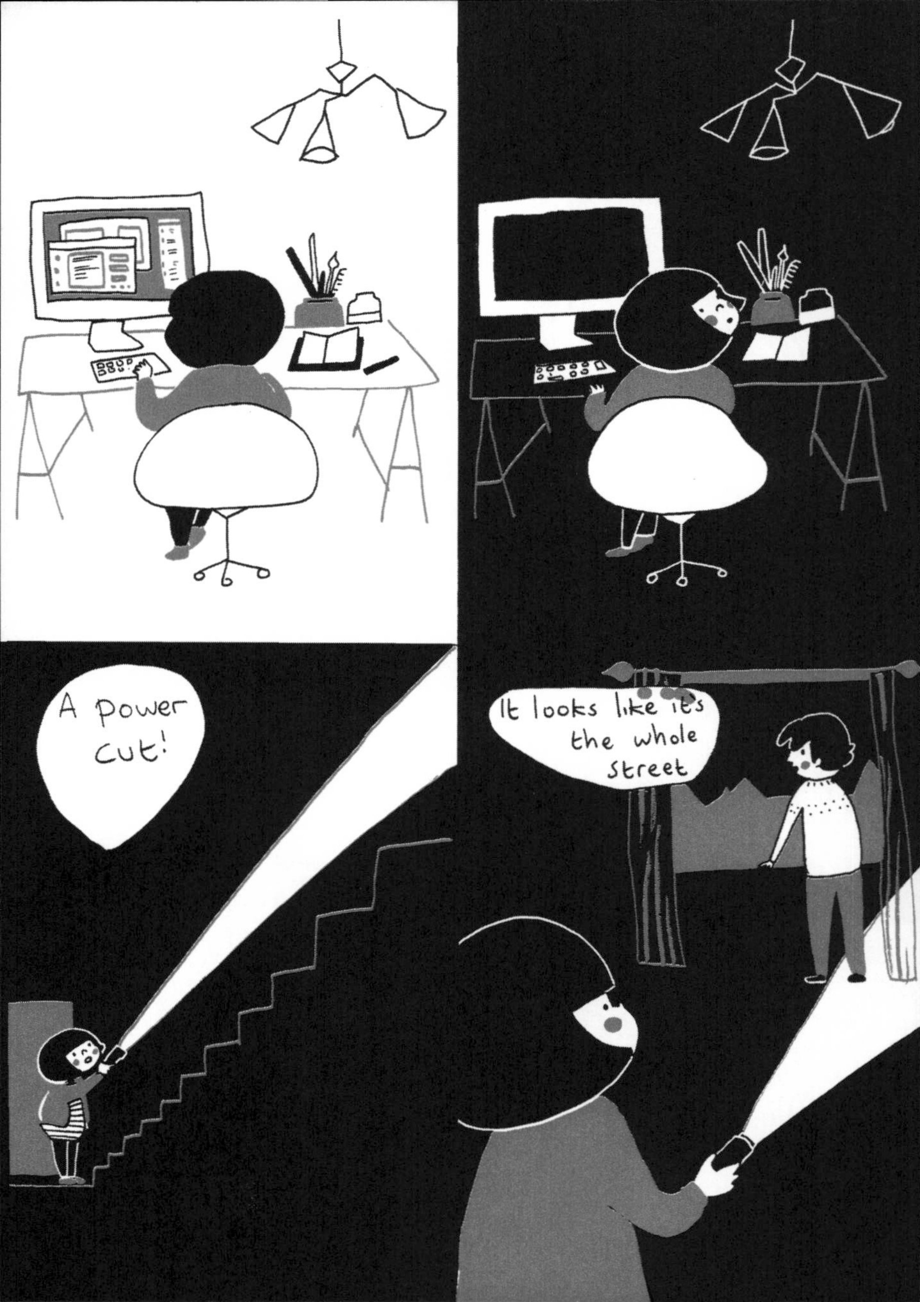
A power cut!
It looks like it's the whole street

We can't work with no lights
Shall we play a board game or something?
oh it's back

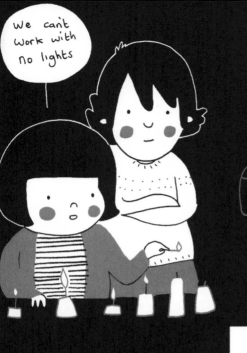

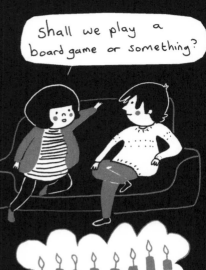

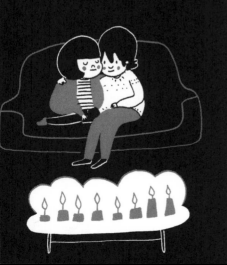

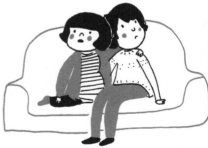

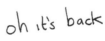

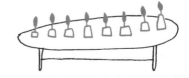

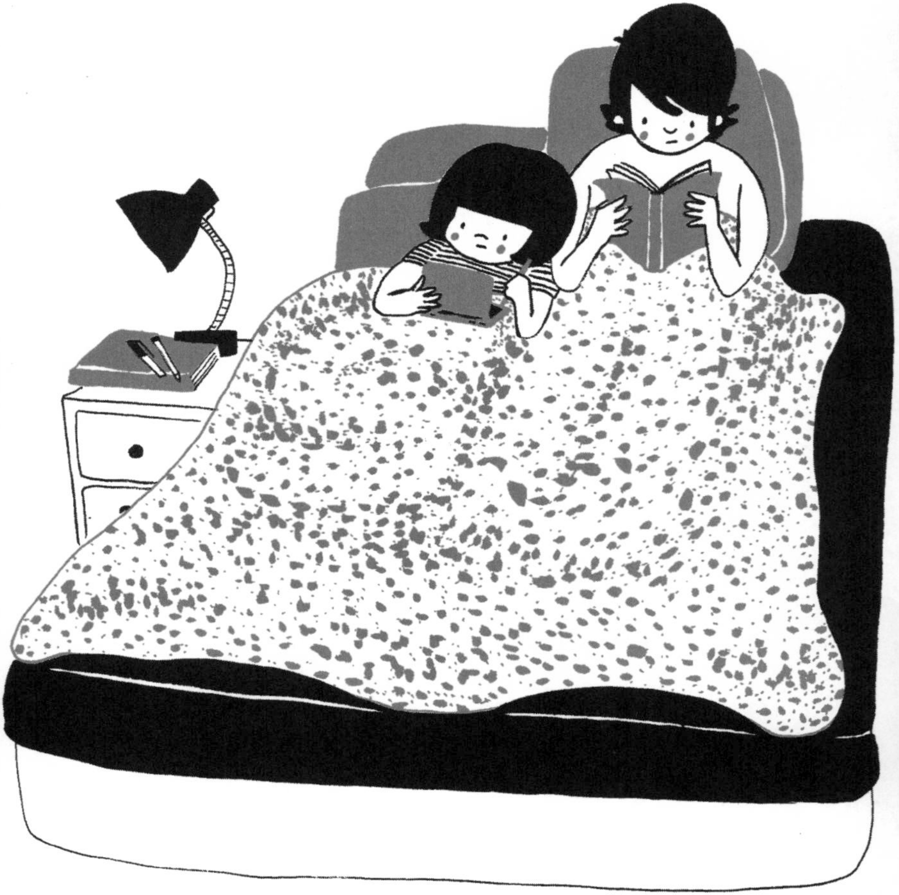

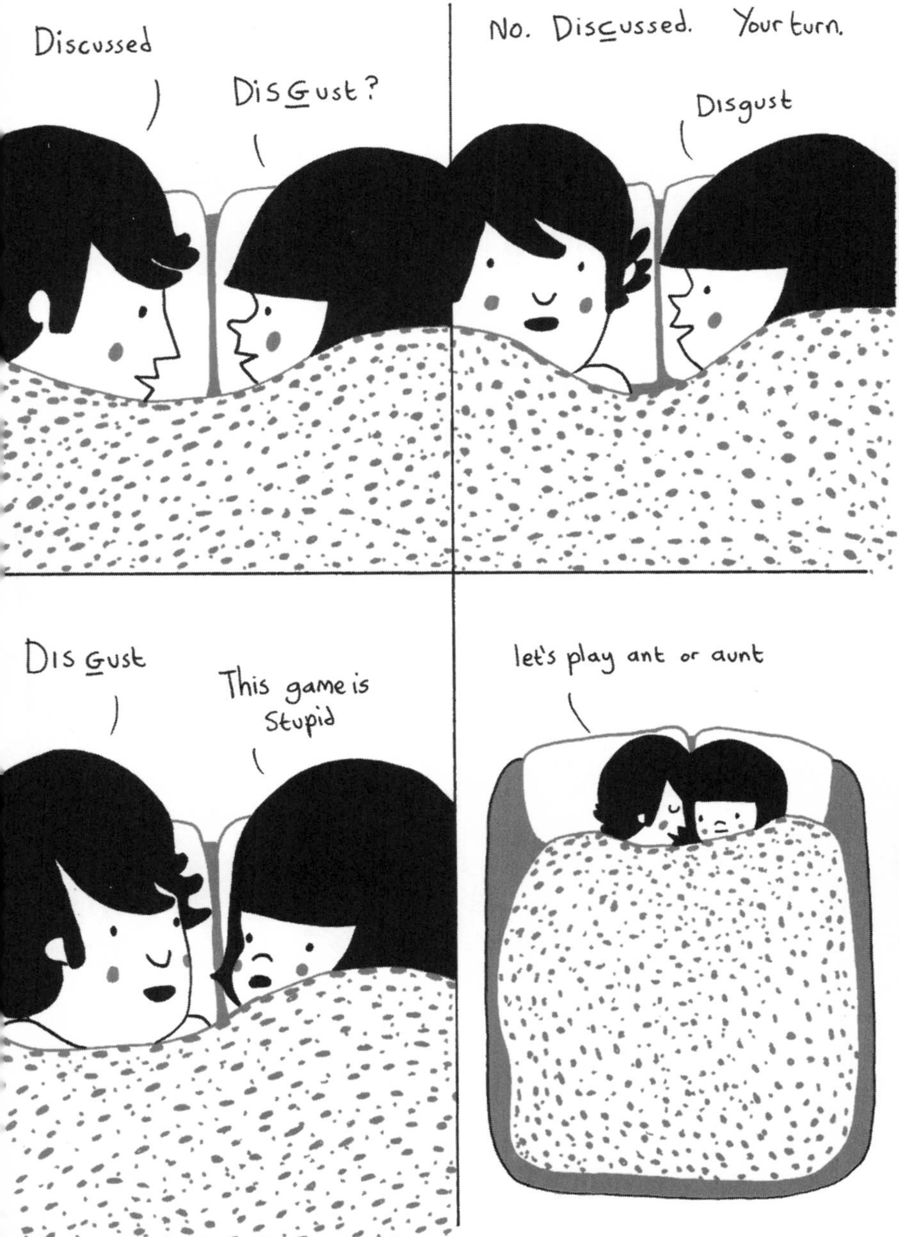
Discussed
DisGust?
No. Discussed. Your turn.
Disgust
DisGust
This game is stupid
let's play ant or aunt

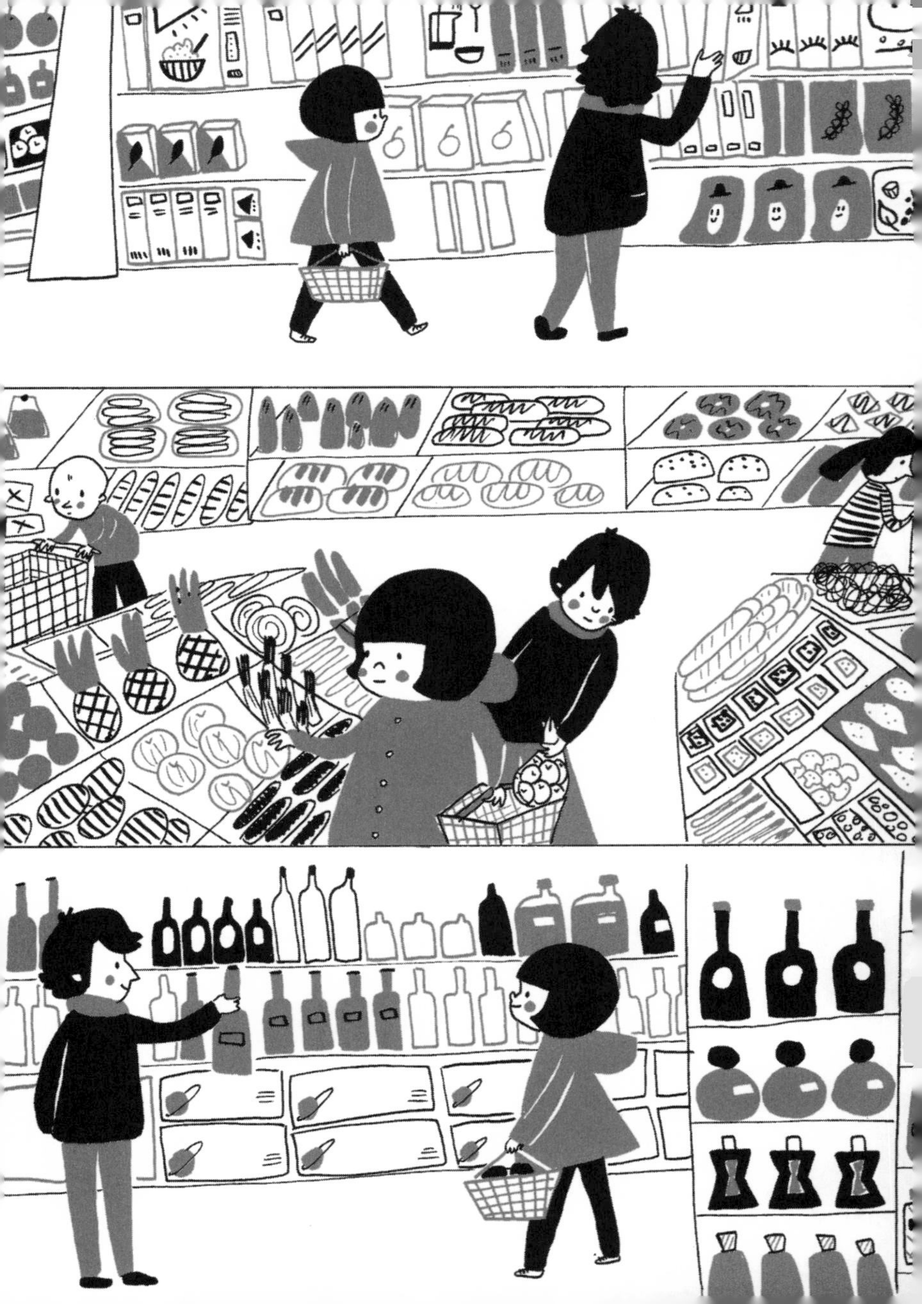

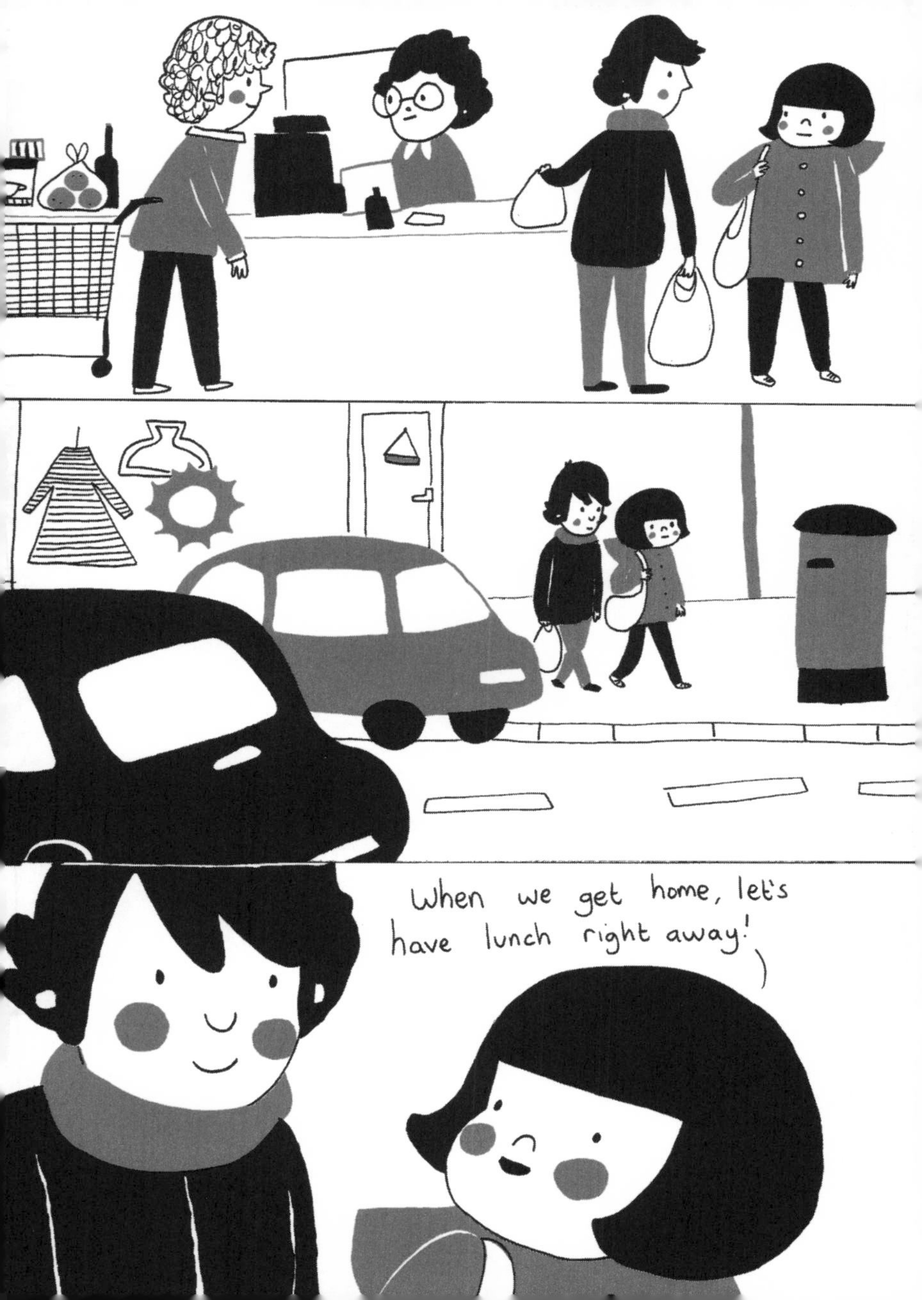
When we get home, let's have lunch right away!

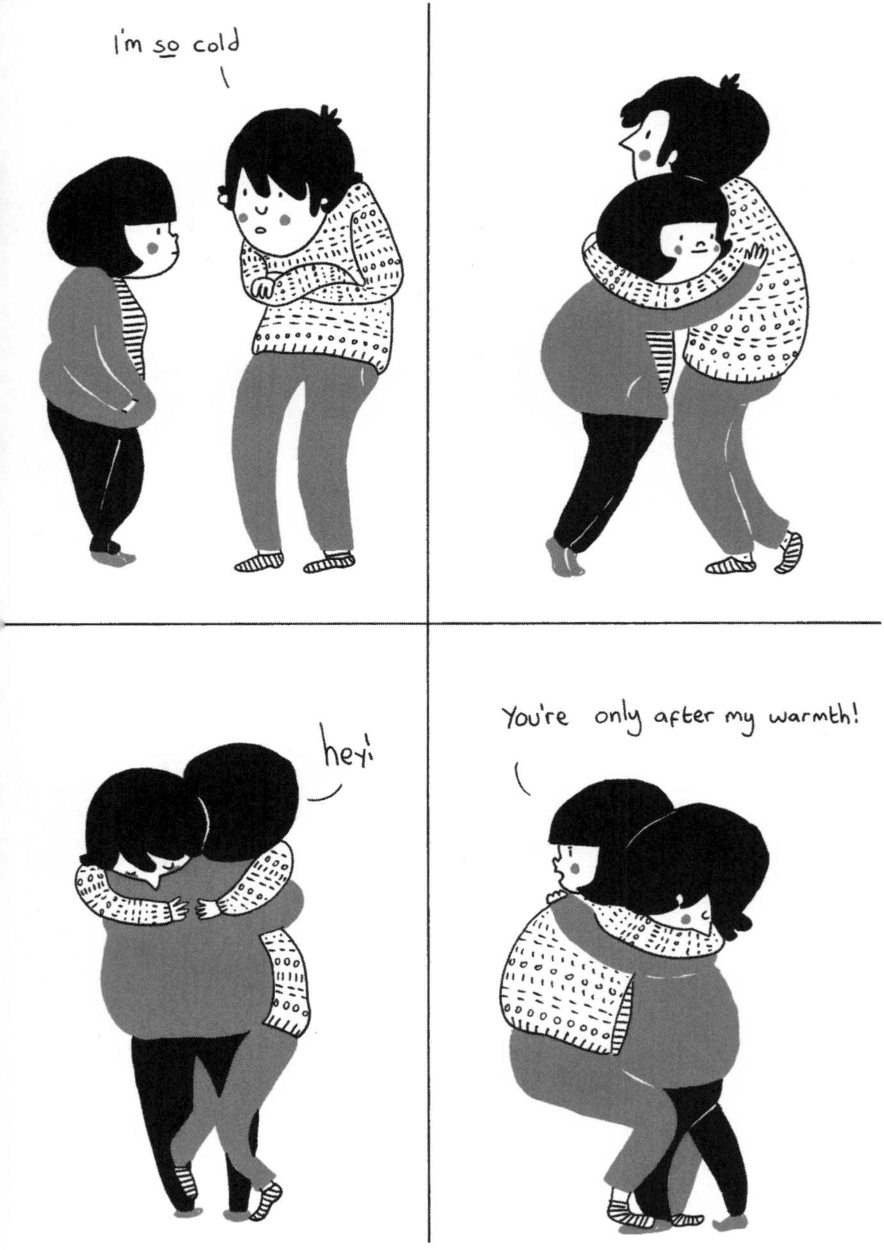
I'm so cold
hey!
You're only after my warmth!

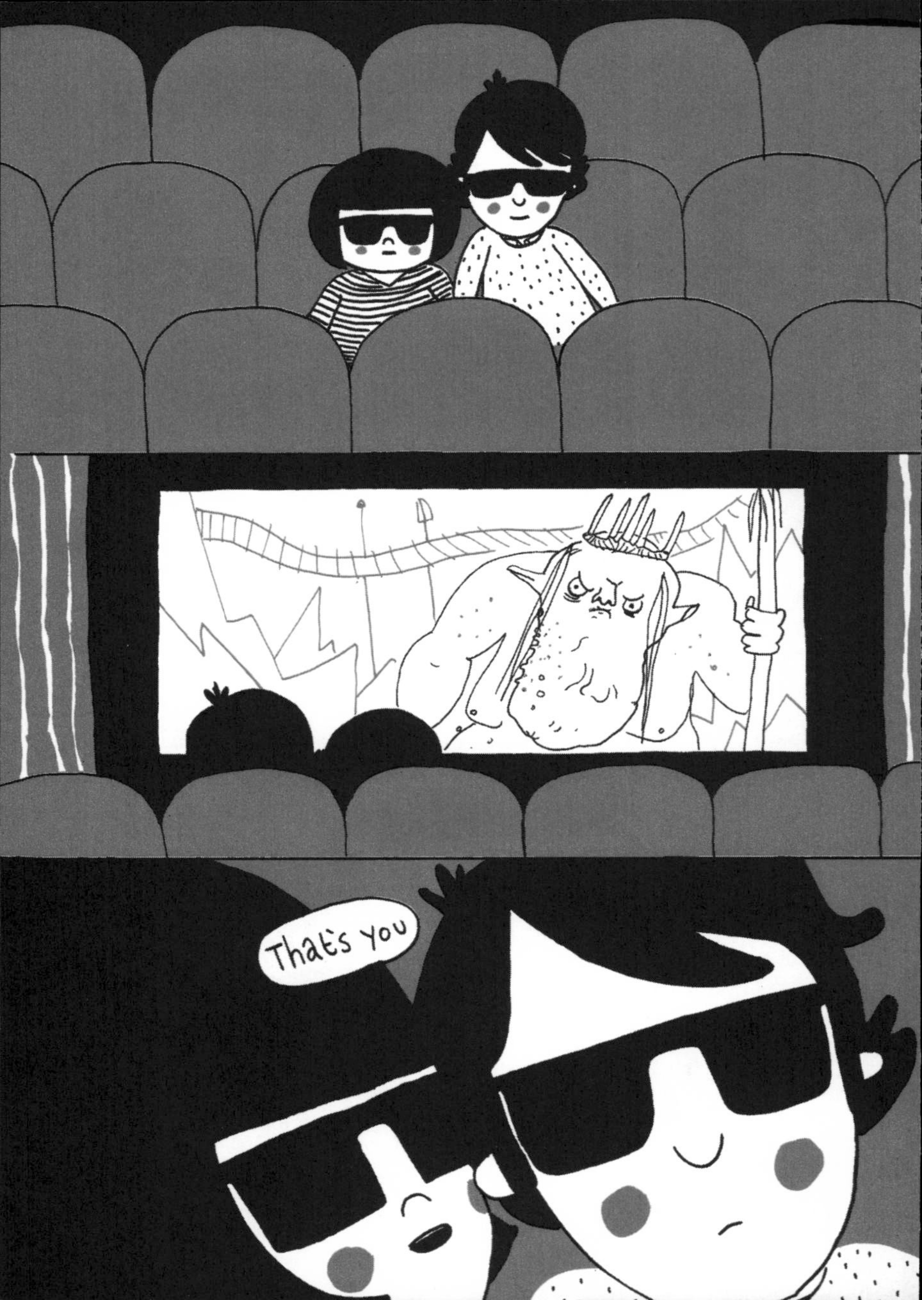
That's you

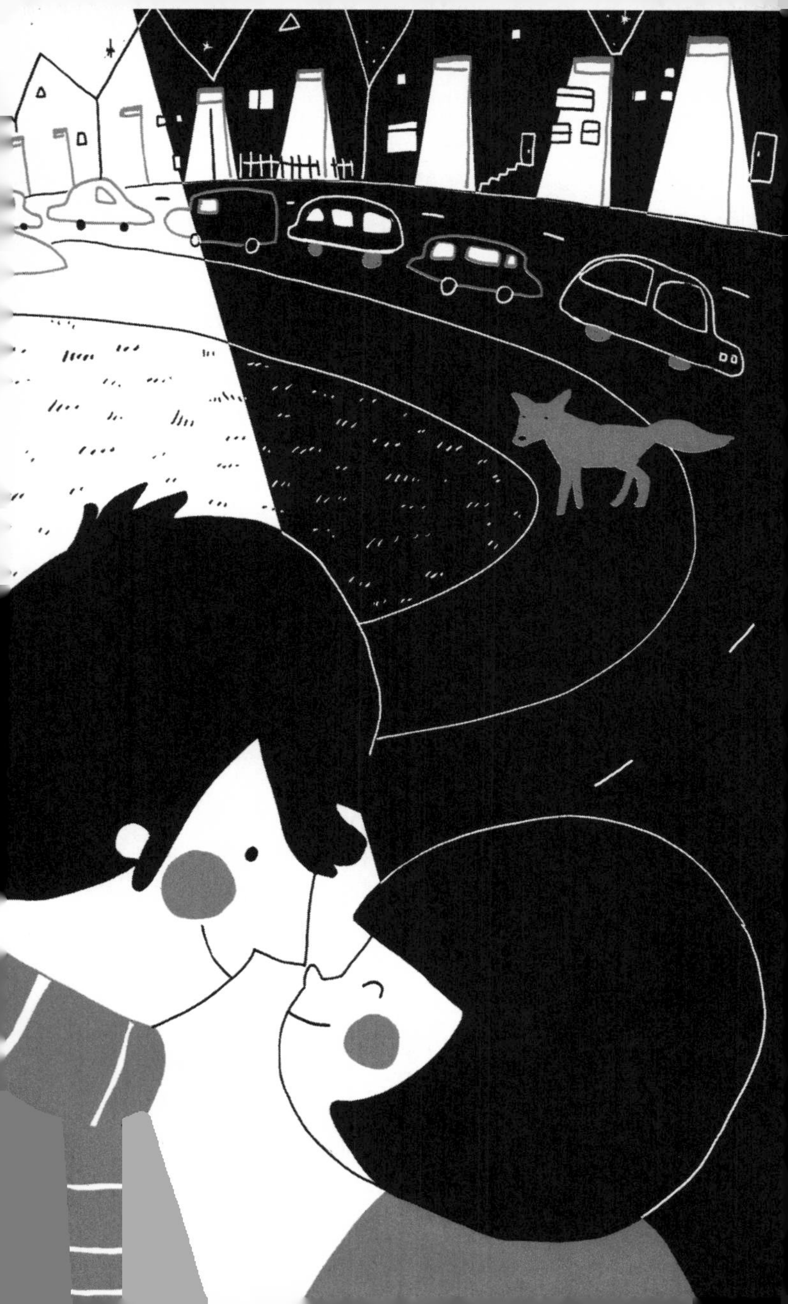

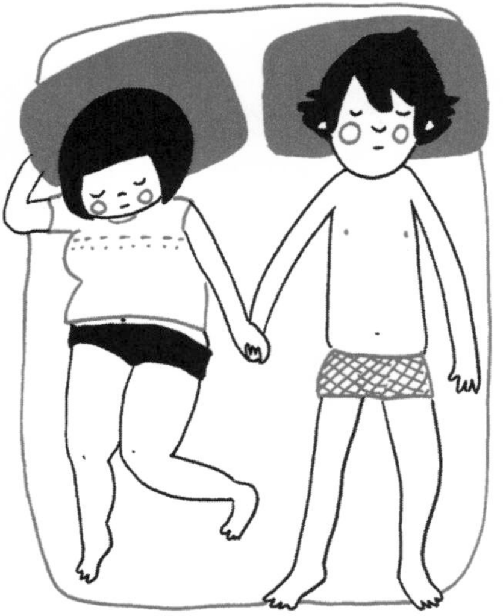

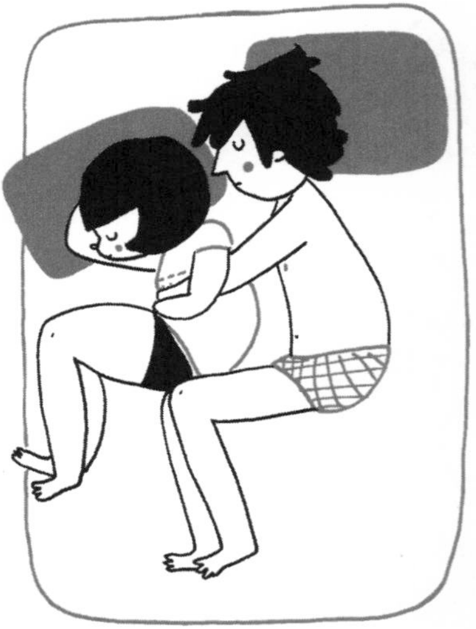

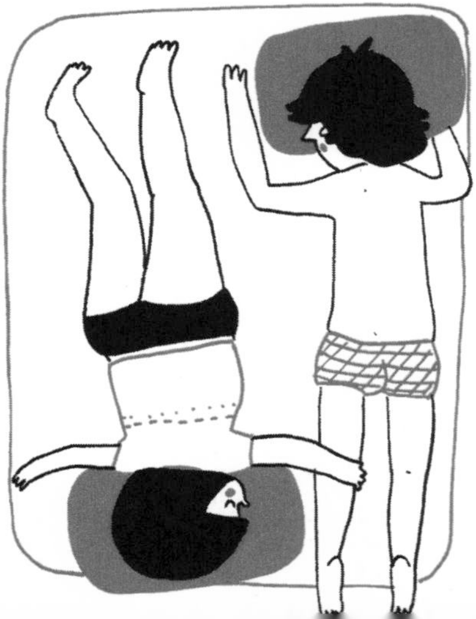

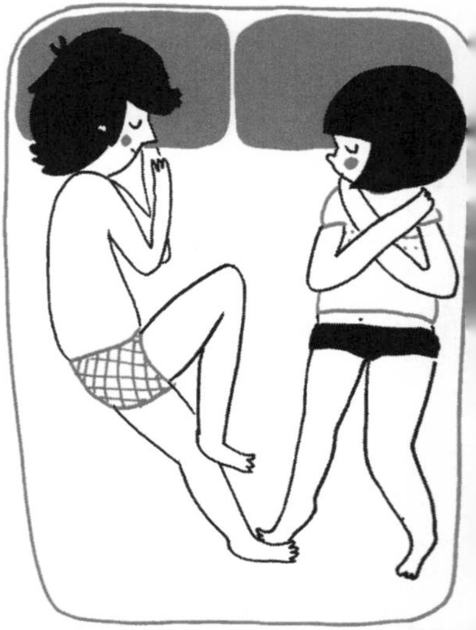

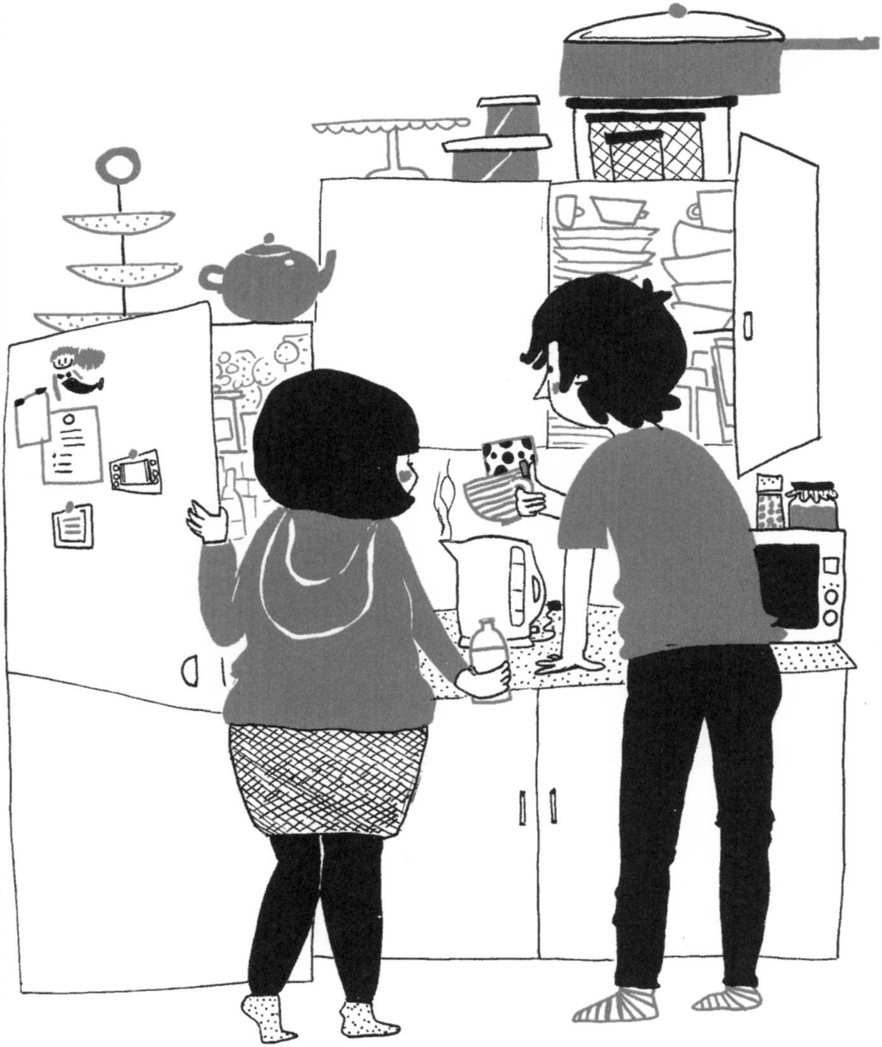

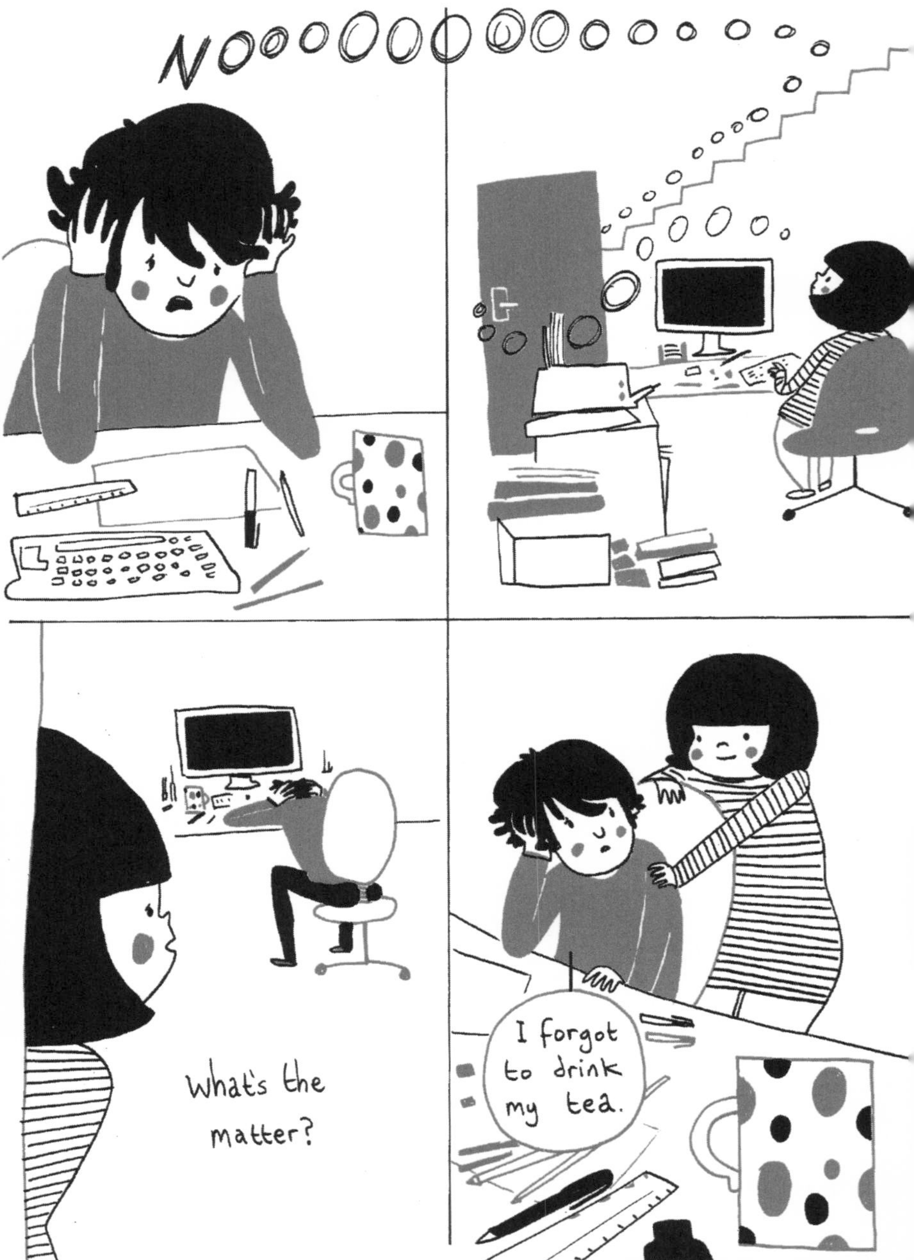
NOooooOOO0OOOOoooooooo
What's the matter?
I forgot to drink my tea.

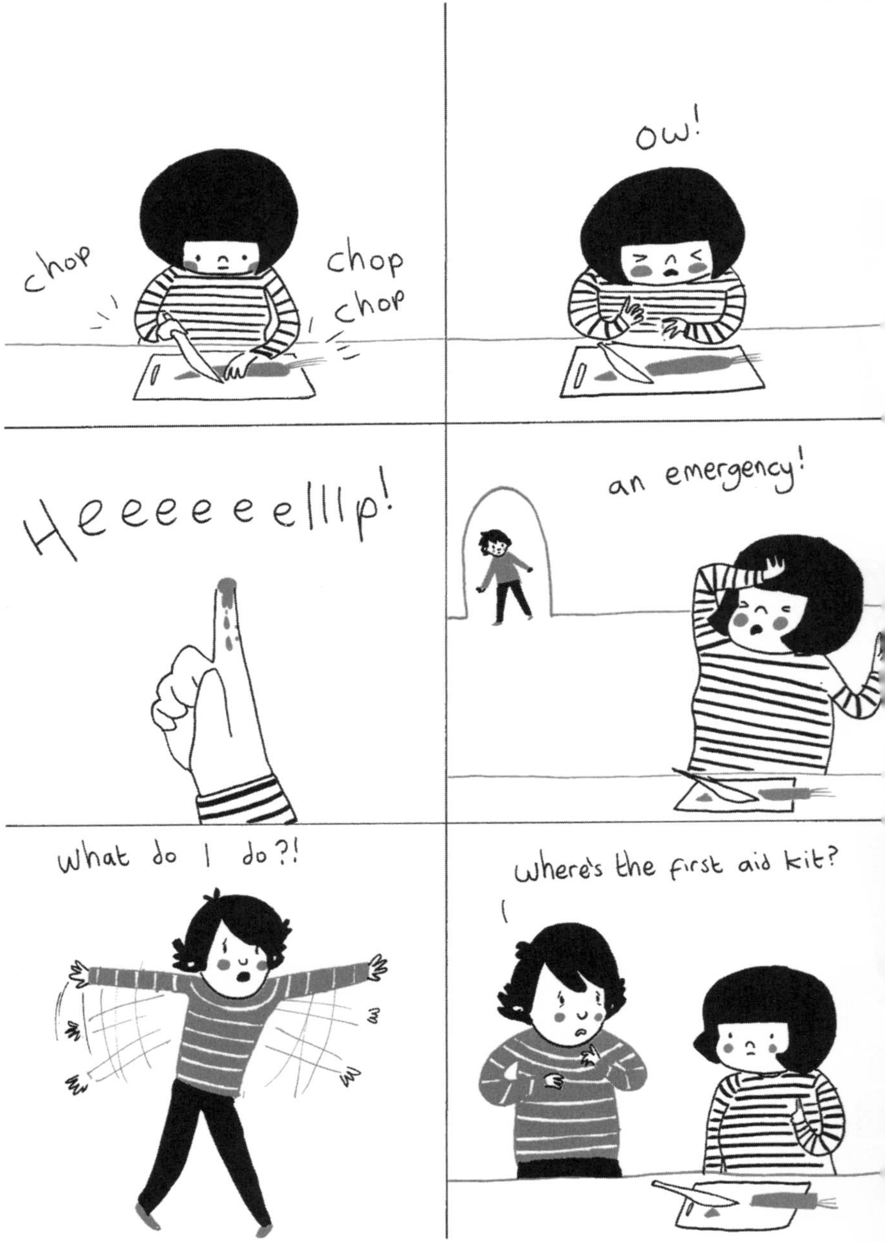
chop
chop chop
ow!
Heeeeeellllp!
an emergency!
what do I do?!
where's the first aid kit?

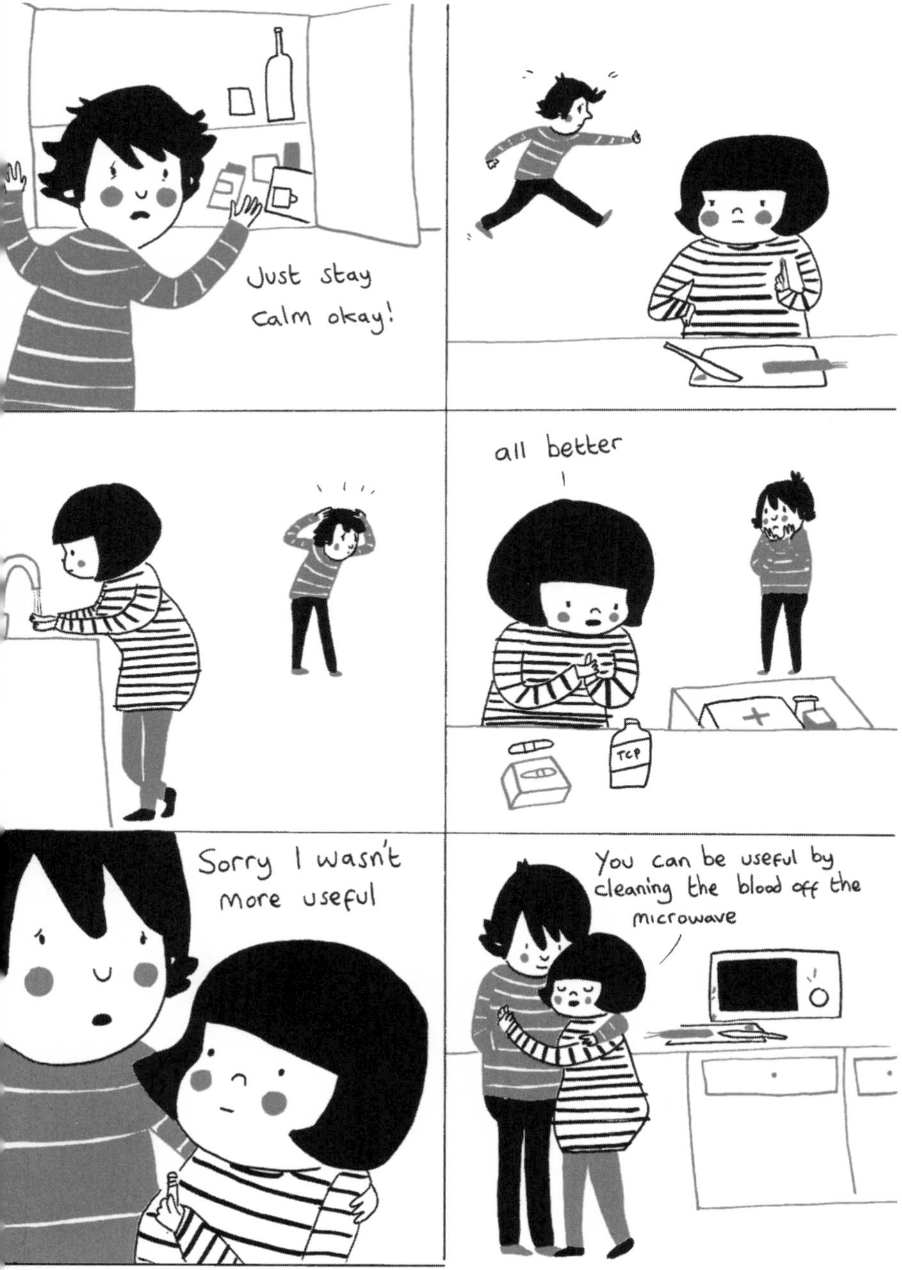
Just stay calm okay!
all better
Sorry I wasn't more useful
You can be useful by cleaning the blood off the microwave
TCP

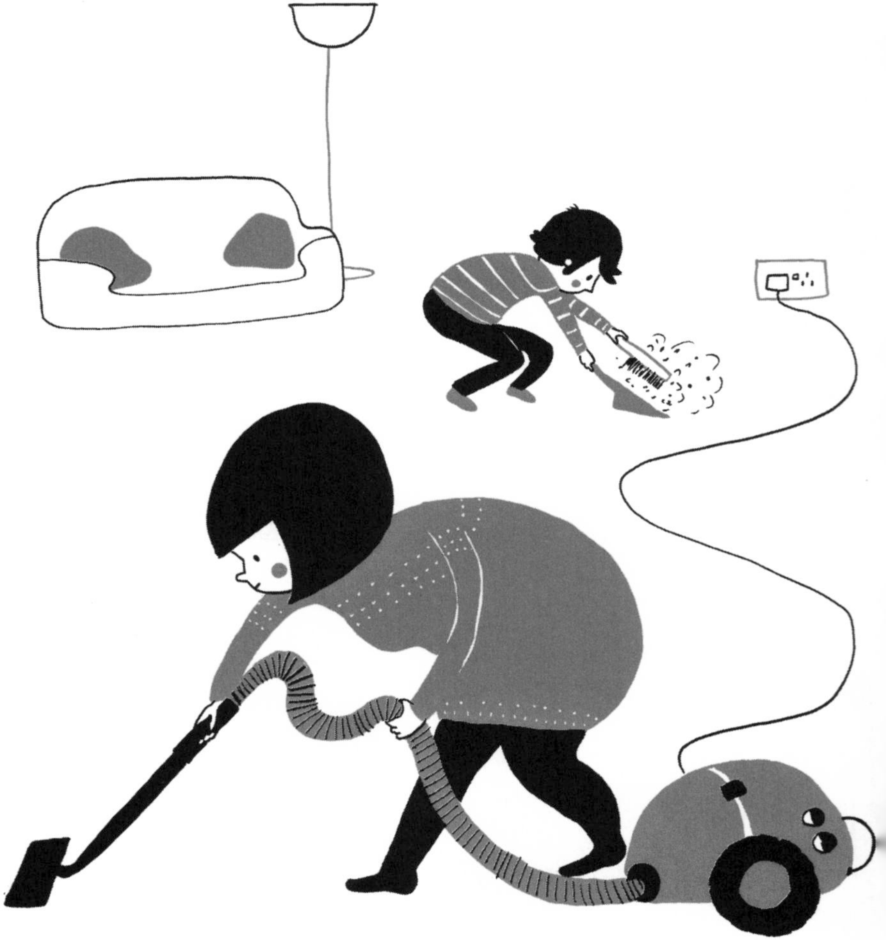

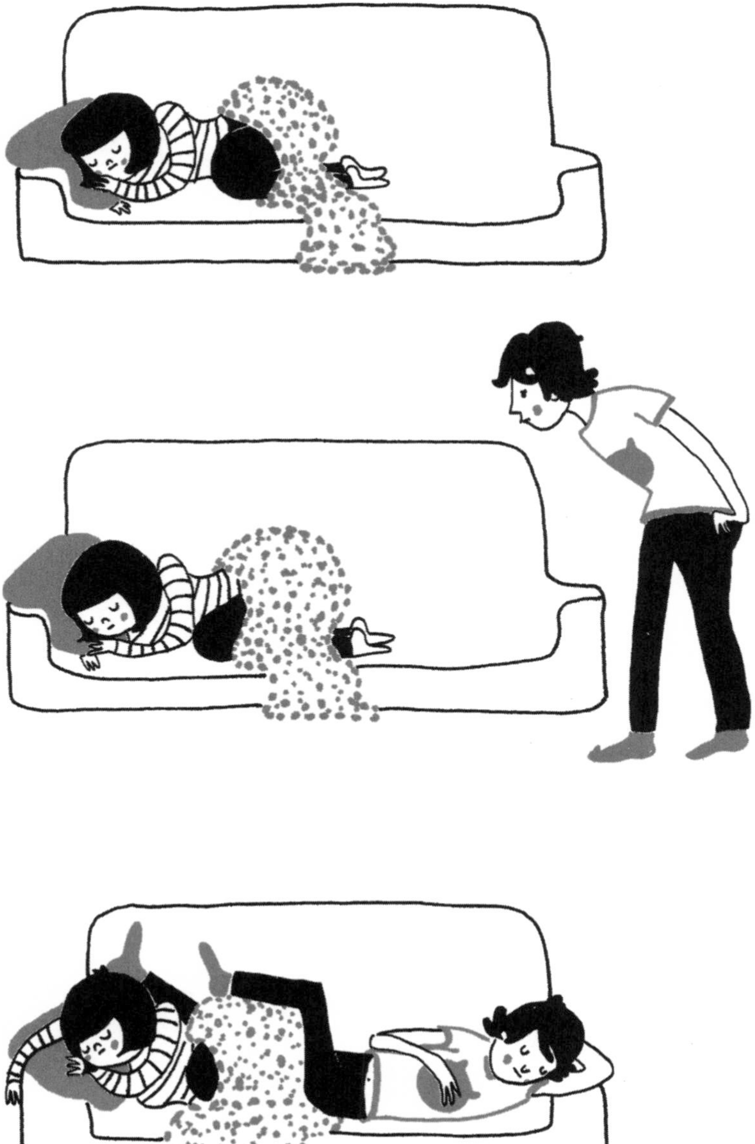

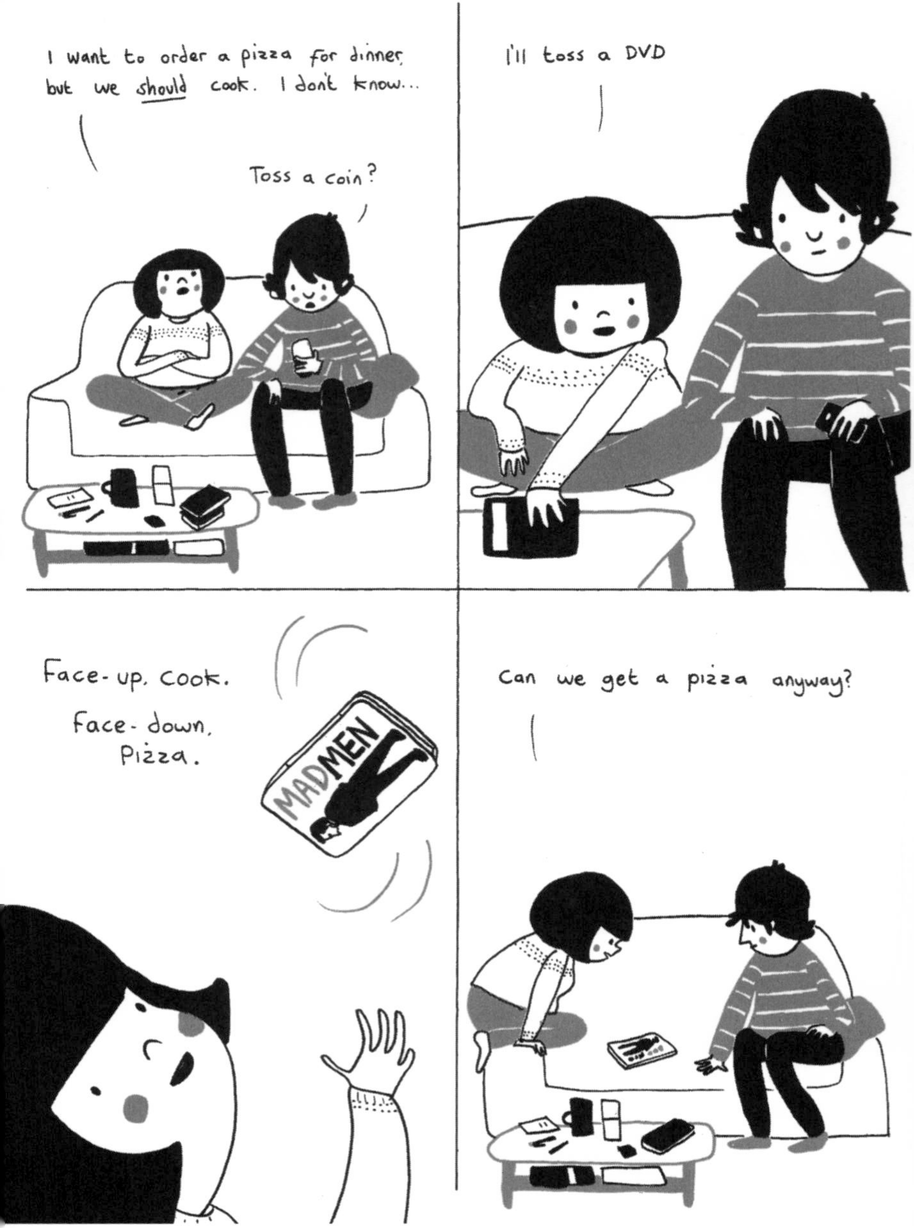
I want to order a pizza for dinner, but we should cook. I don't know...
Toss a coin?
I'll toss a DVD
Face-up, cook.
Face-down, Pizza.
MADMEN
Can we get a pizza anyway?

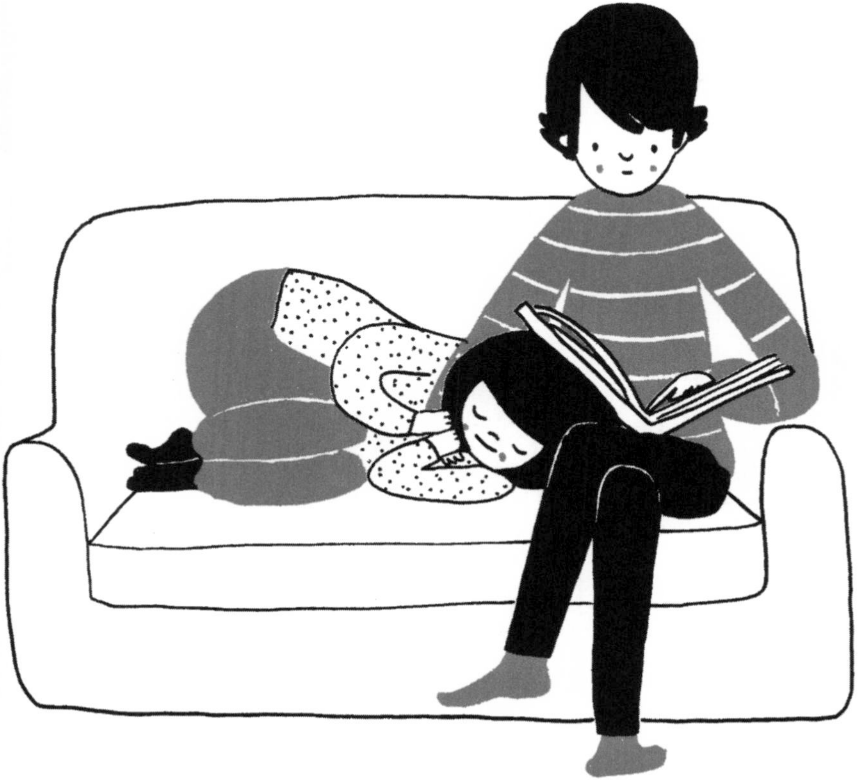

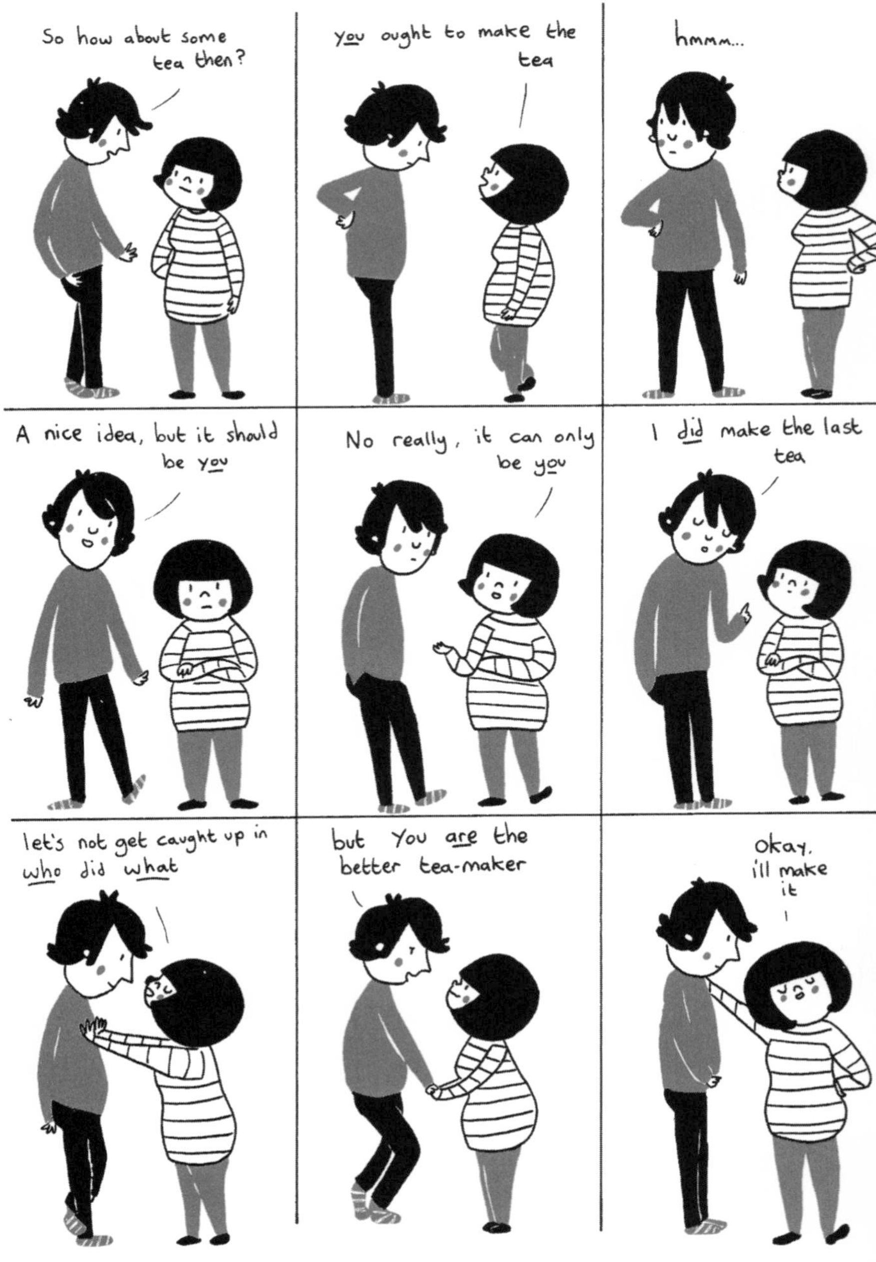
So how about some tea then?
you ought to make the tea
hmmm...
A nice idea, but it should be you
No really, it can only be you
I did make the last tea
let's not get caught up in who did what
but You are the better tea-maker
Okay, ill make it

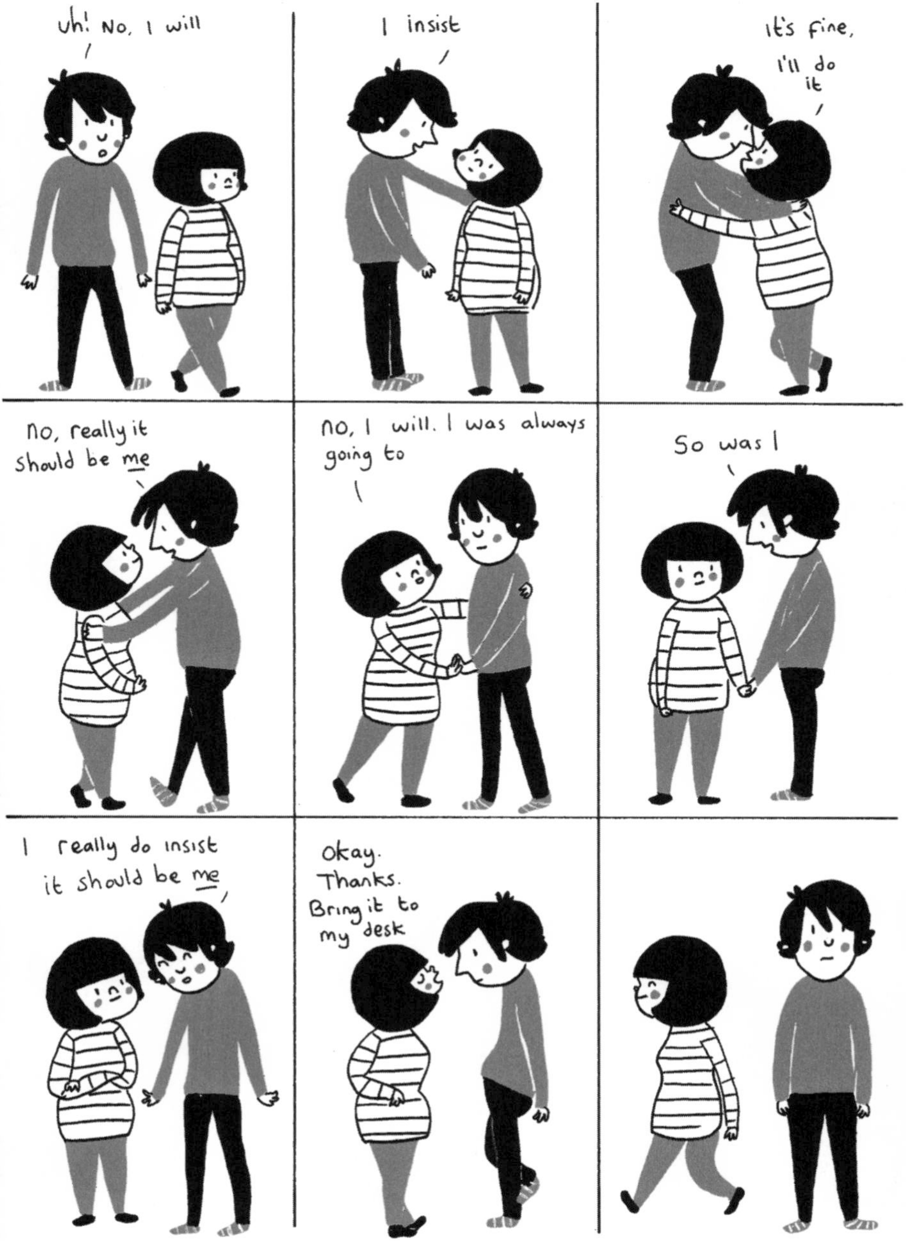

uh! No, I will
I insist
It's fine,
I'll do it
No, really it should be me
No, I will. I was always going to
So was I
I really do insist it should be me
Okay. Thanks. Bring it to my desk

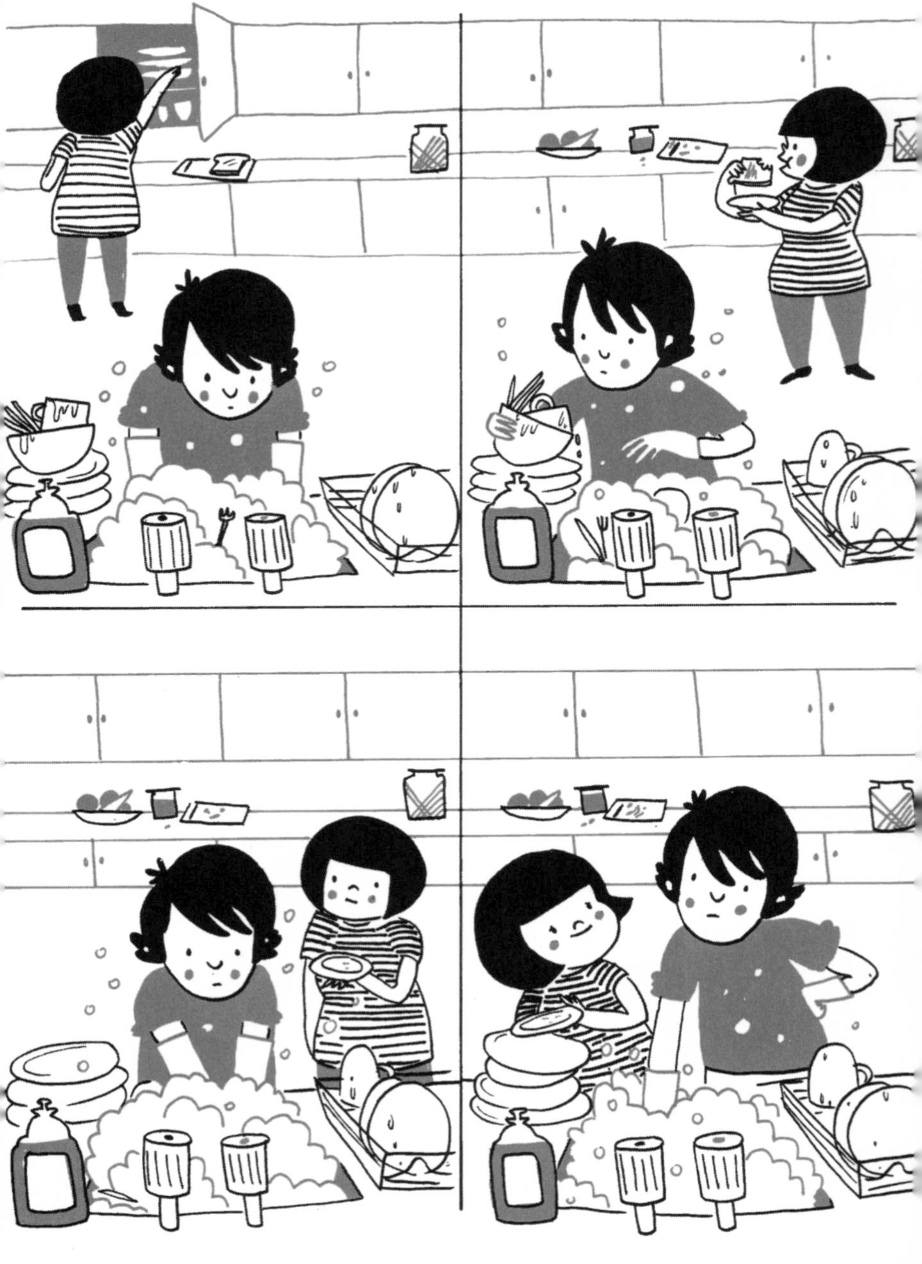

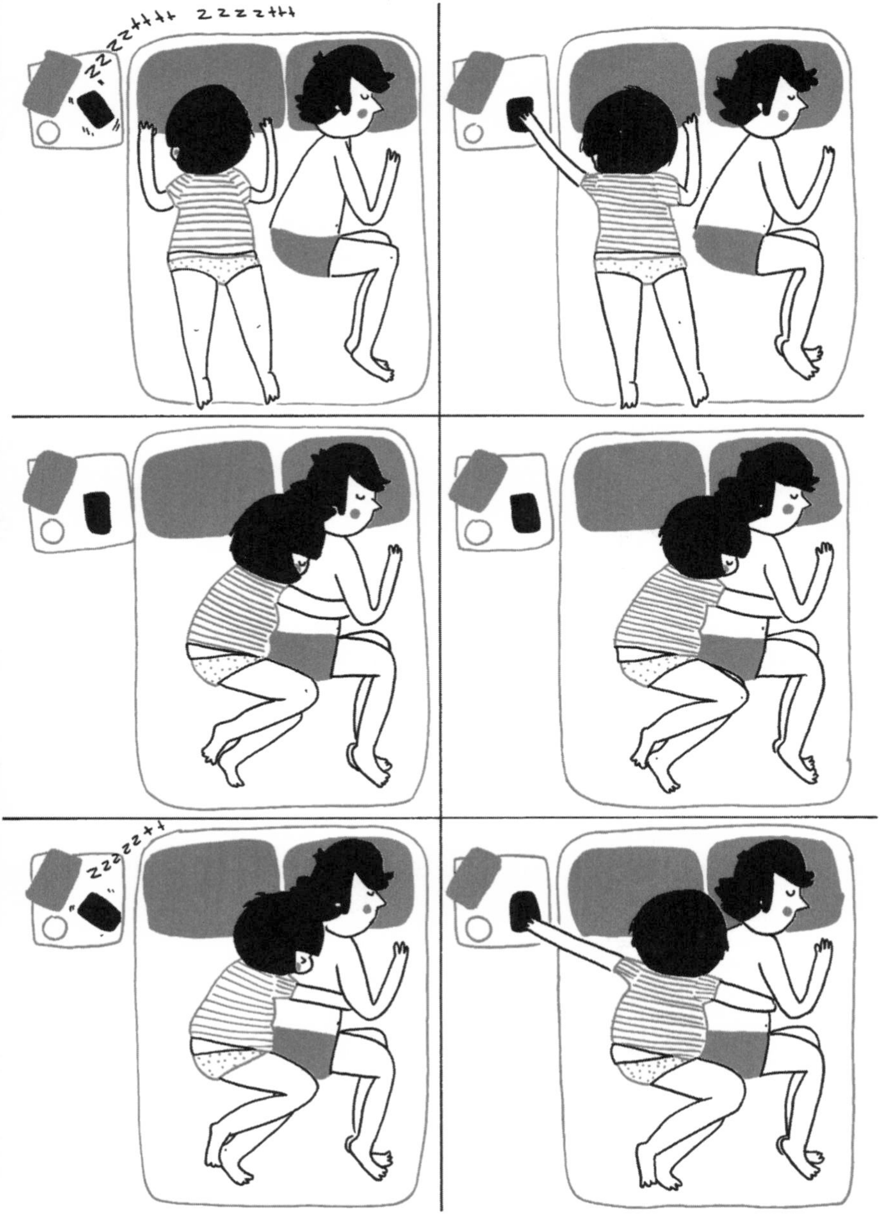

ZZZZtttt ZZZZttt
ZZZZZtt

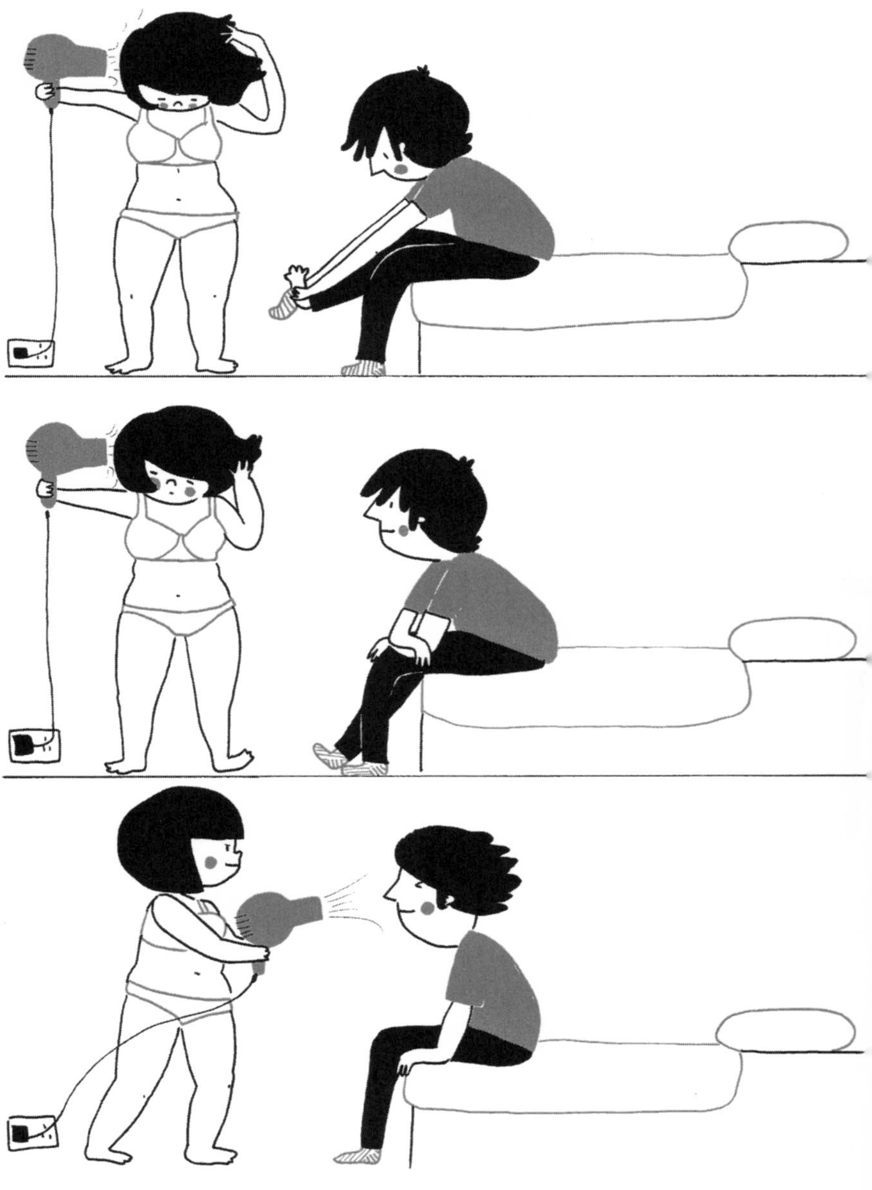

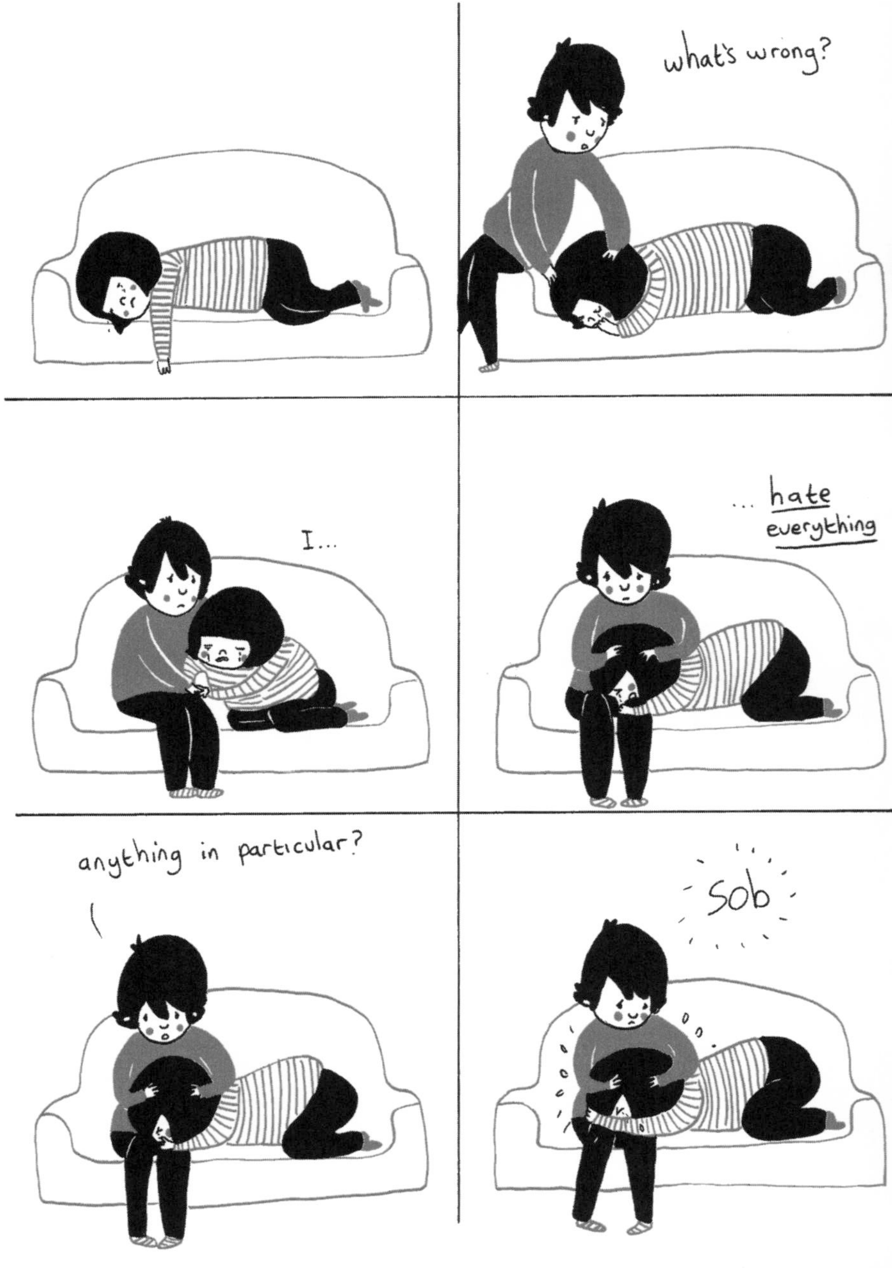
what's wrong?
I...
... hate everything
anything in particular?
sob

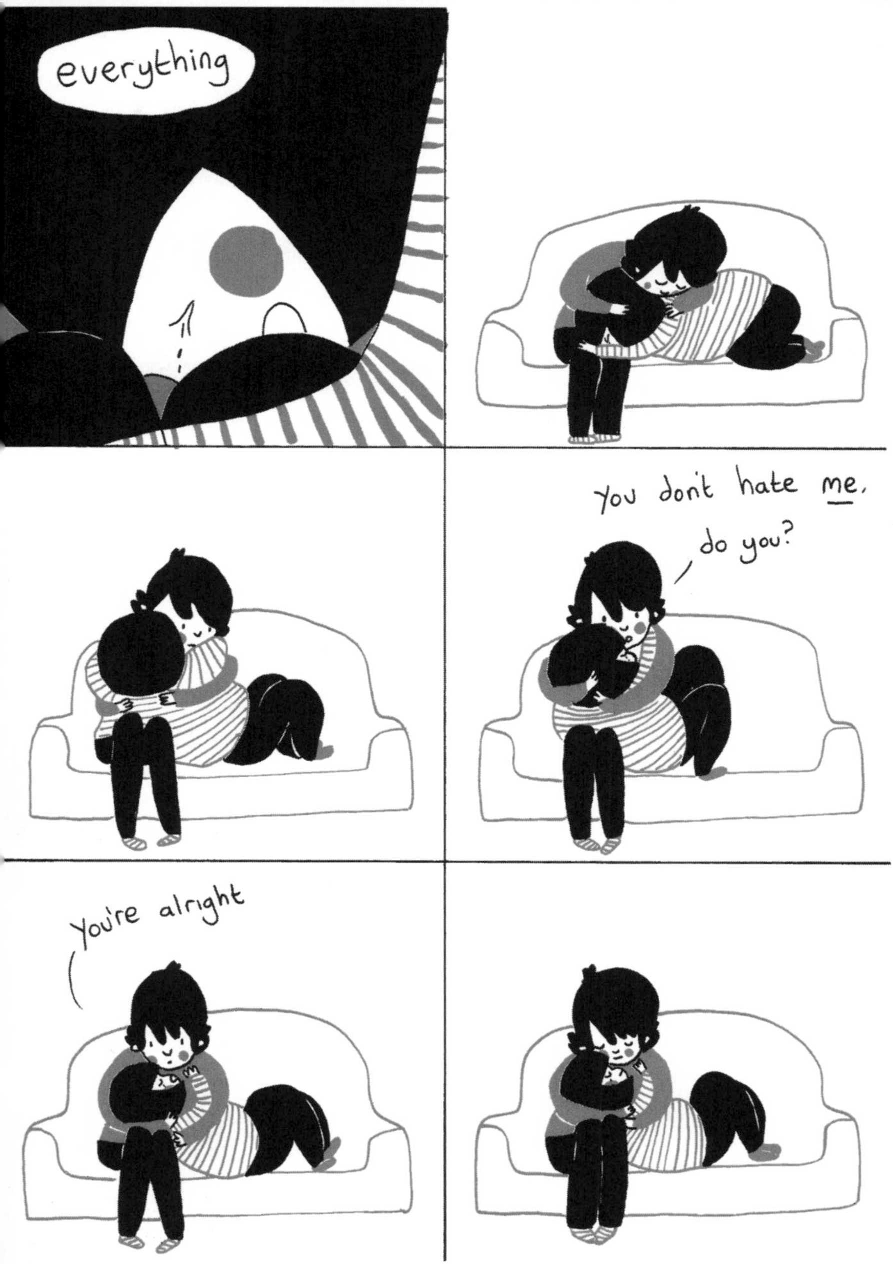
everything
You don't hate me,
do you?
You're alright

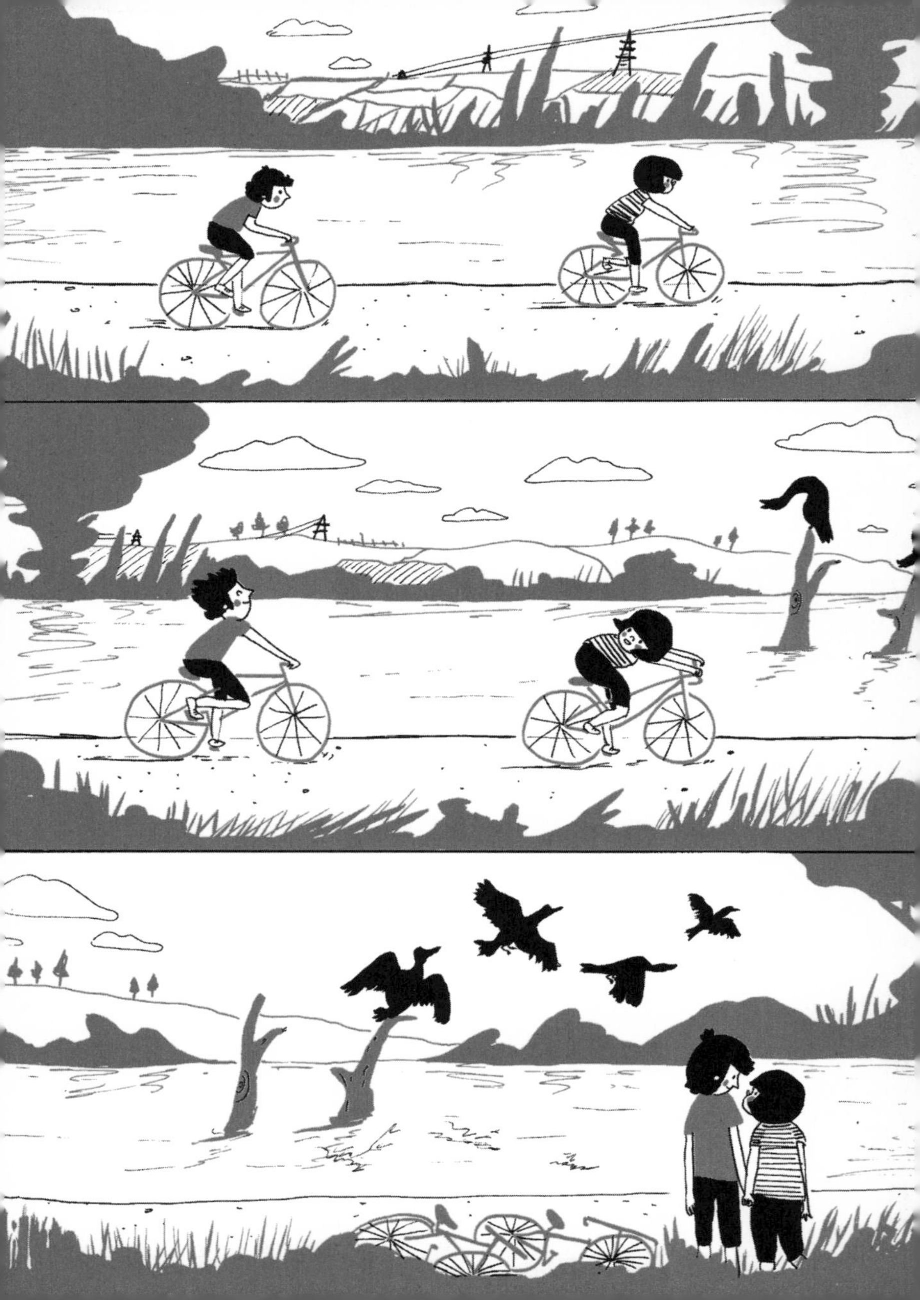

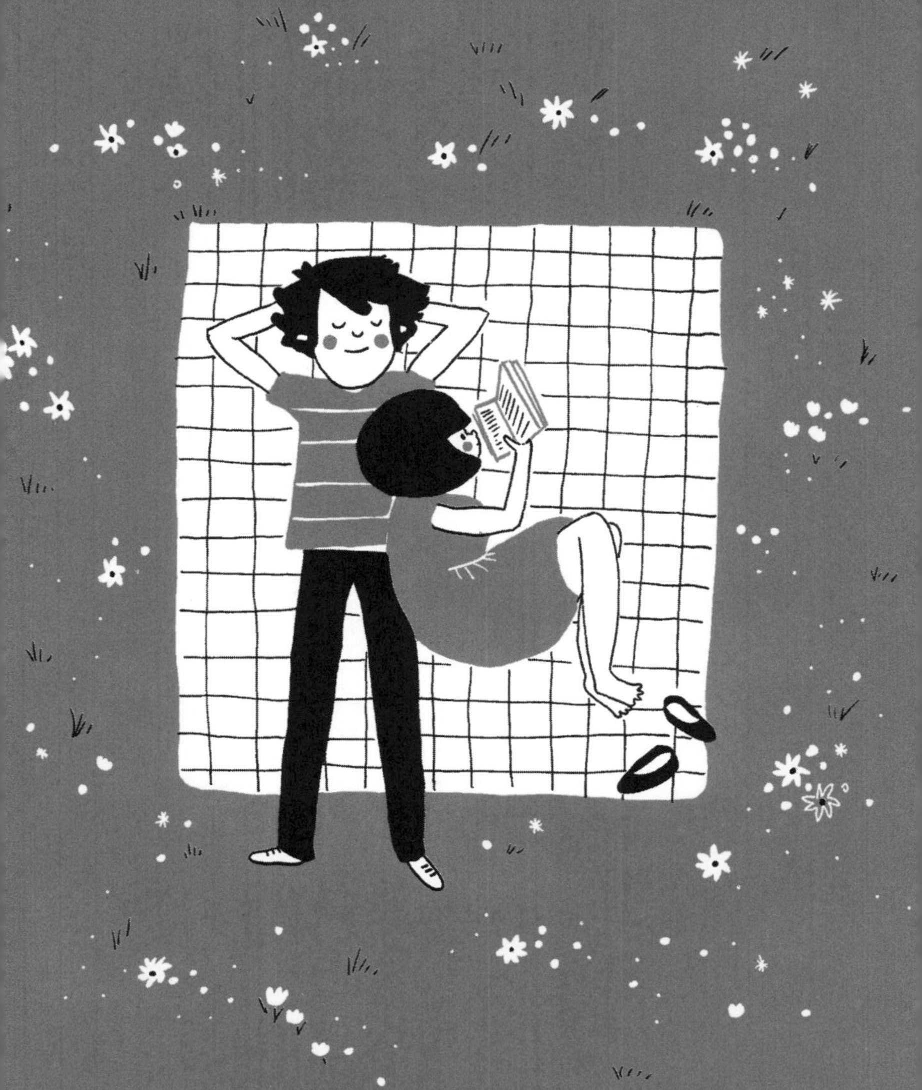

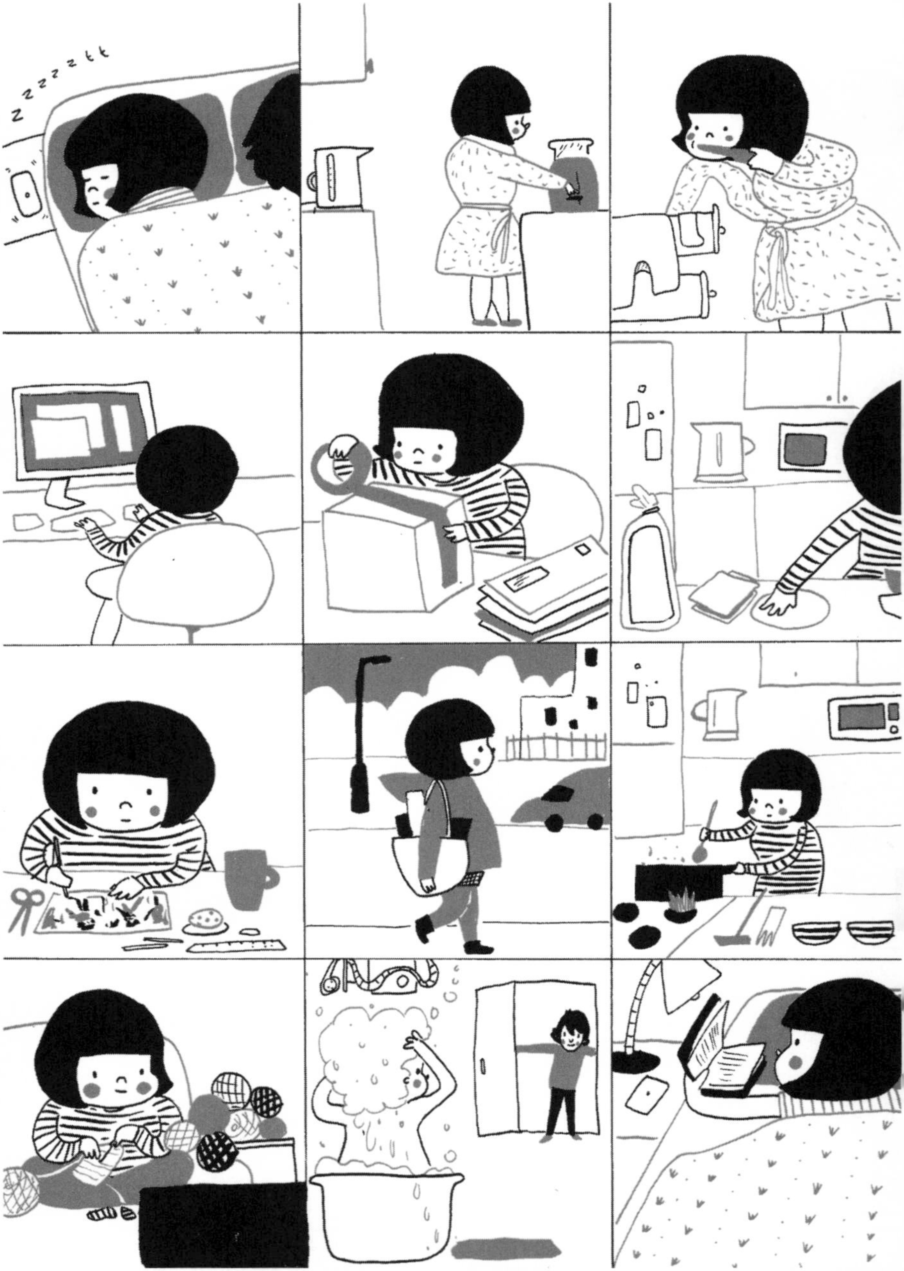
zzzzzzzz

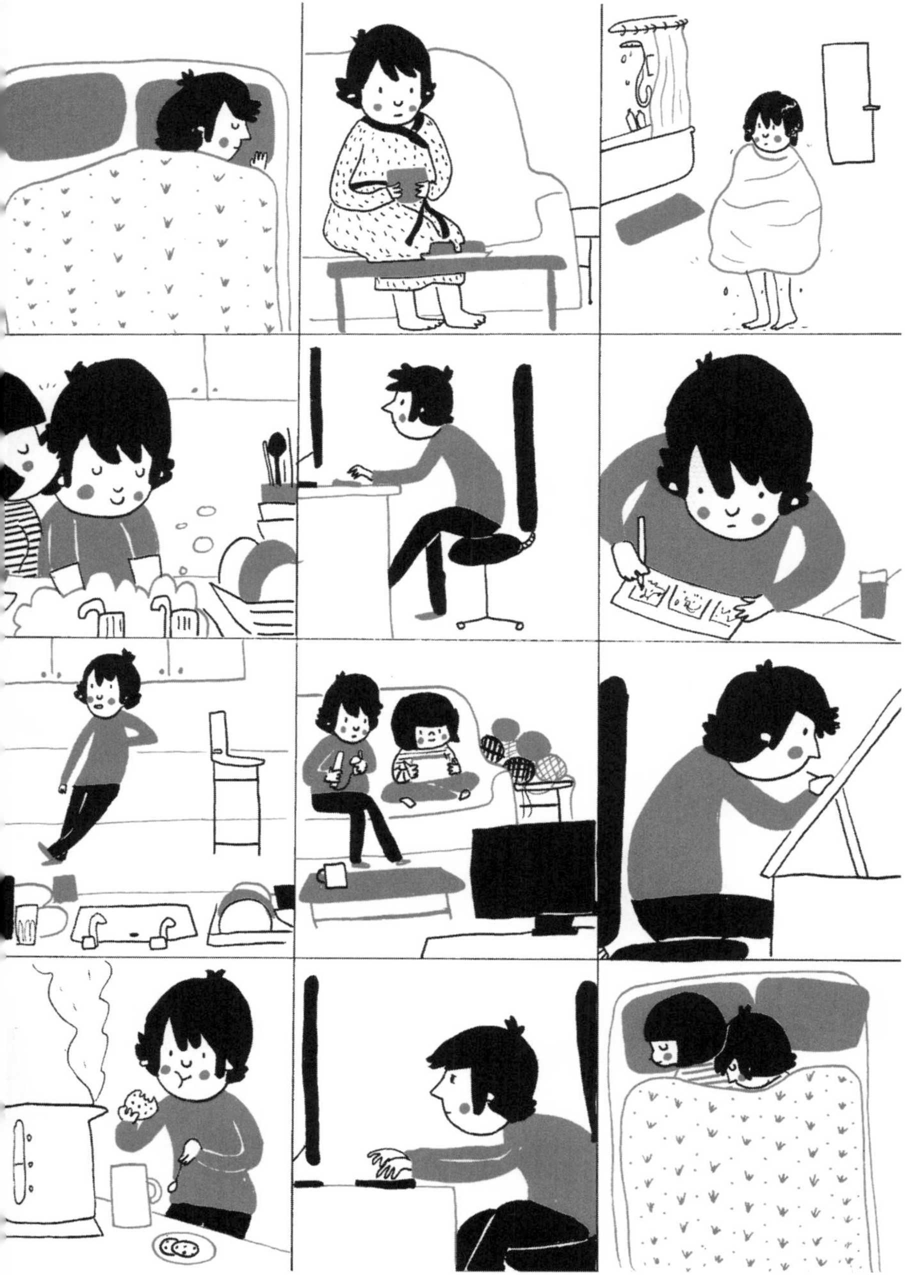

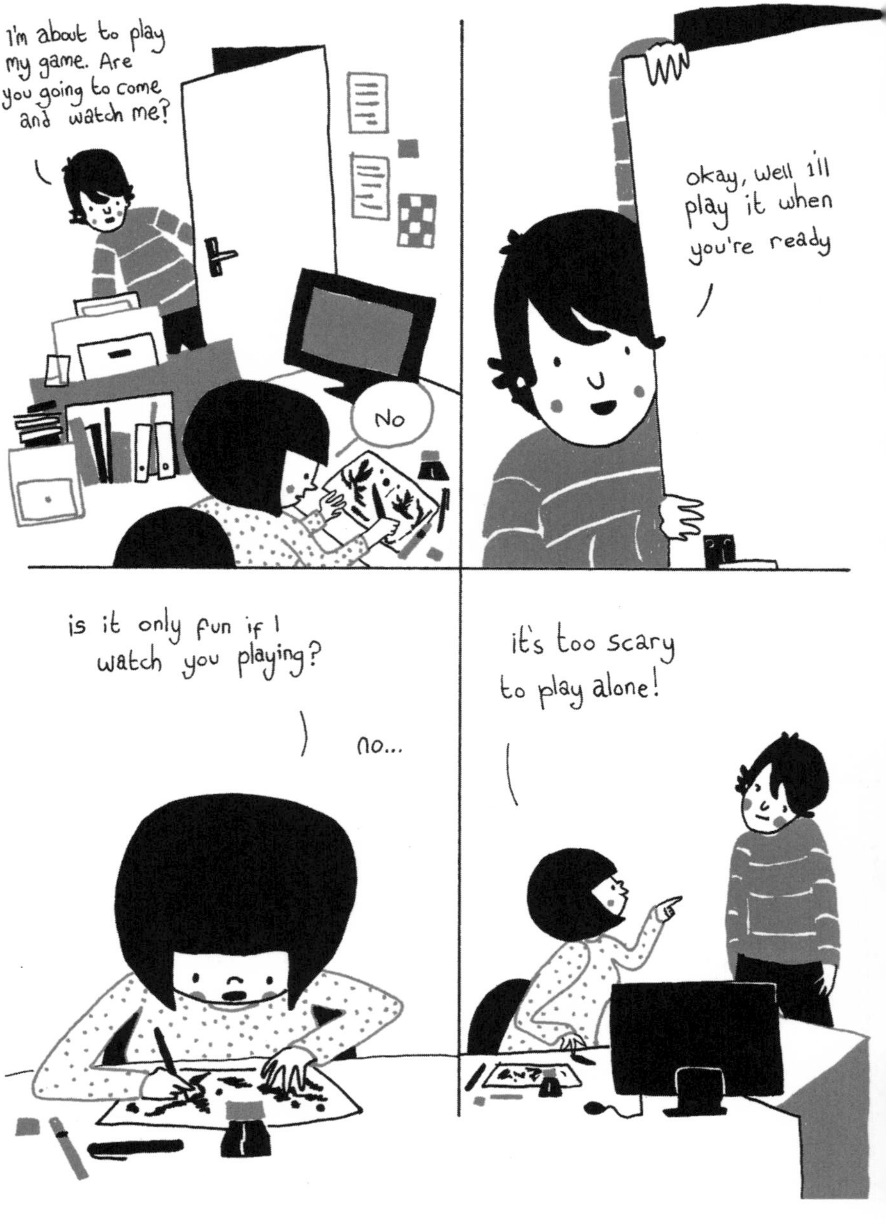
I'm about to play my game. Are you going to come and watch me?
No
okay, well I'll play it when you're ready
is it only fun if I watch you playing?
no...
it's too scary to play alone!

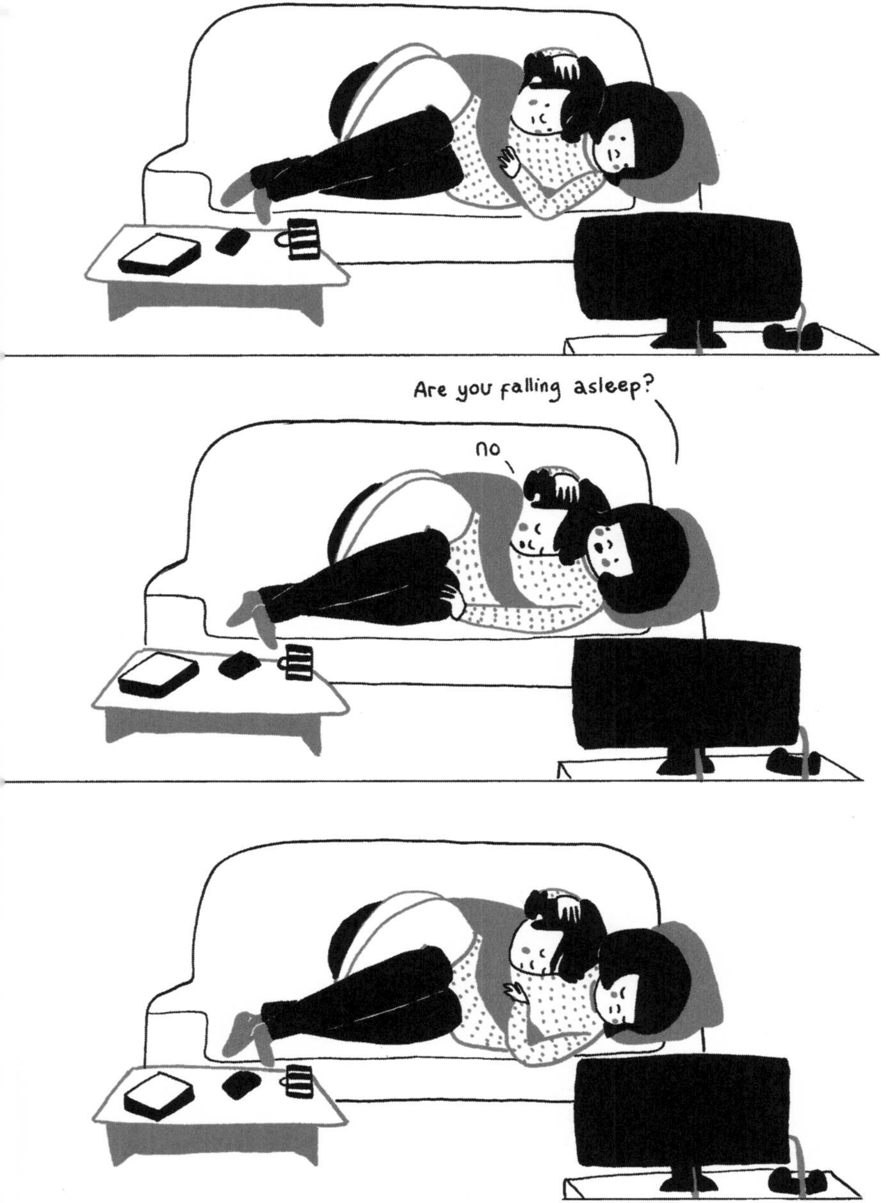
Are you falling asleep?
no

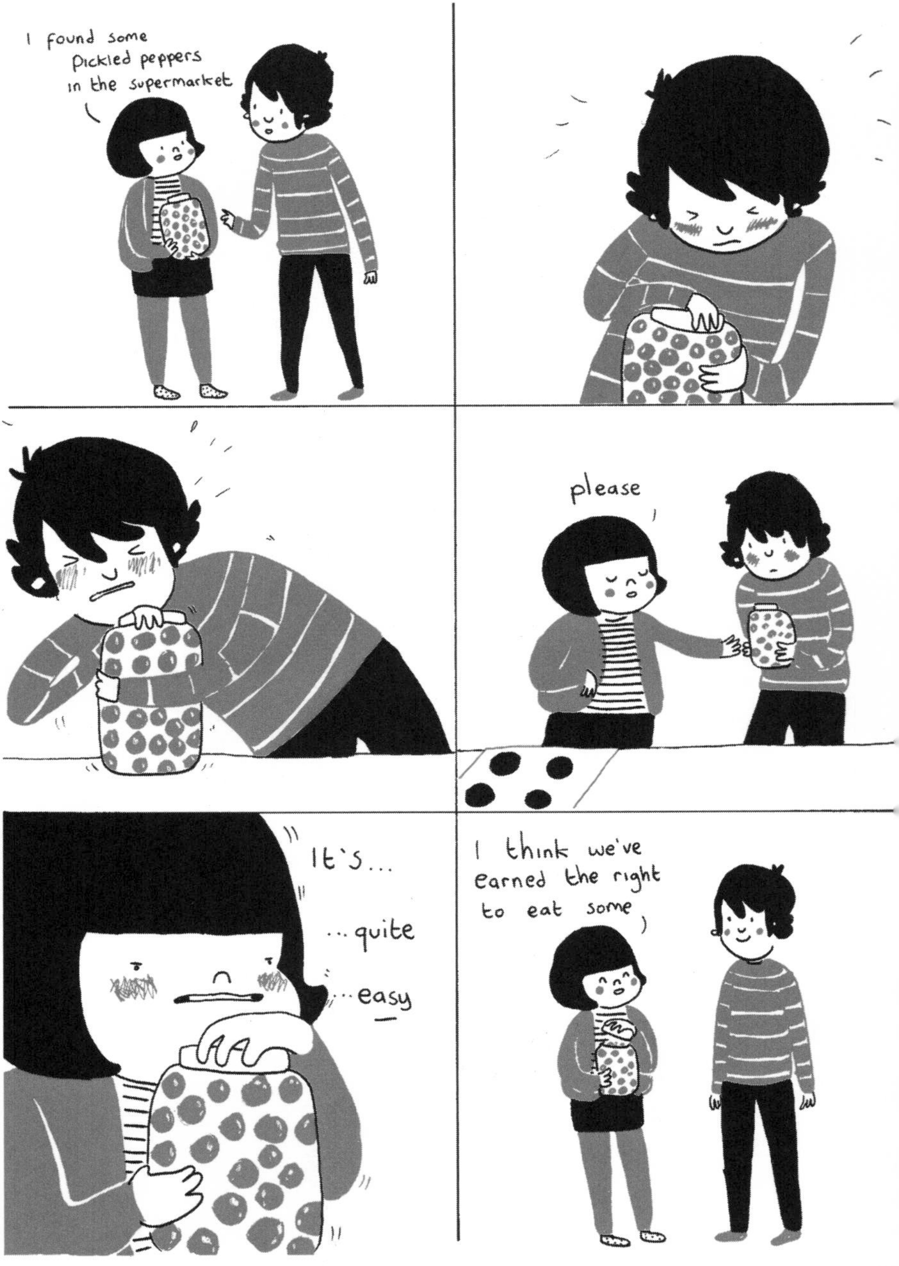
I found some pickled peppers in the supermarket
please
It's...
...quite
...easy
I think we've earned the right to eat some

I'll cook if you wash up

If you phone for the pizza, I'll answer the door when it arrives

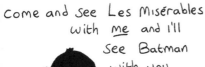

Come and see Les Misérables with me and I'll see Batman with you

let me in!
No!
Stop it! You're letting the cold in

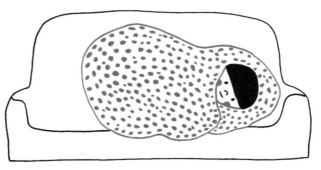

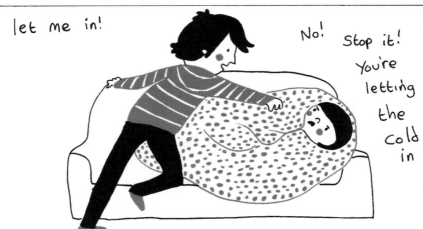

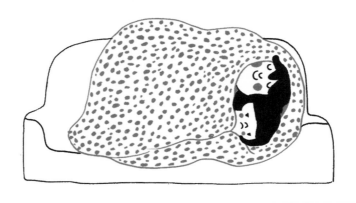

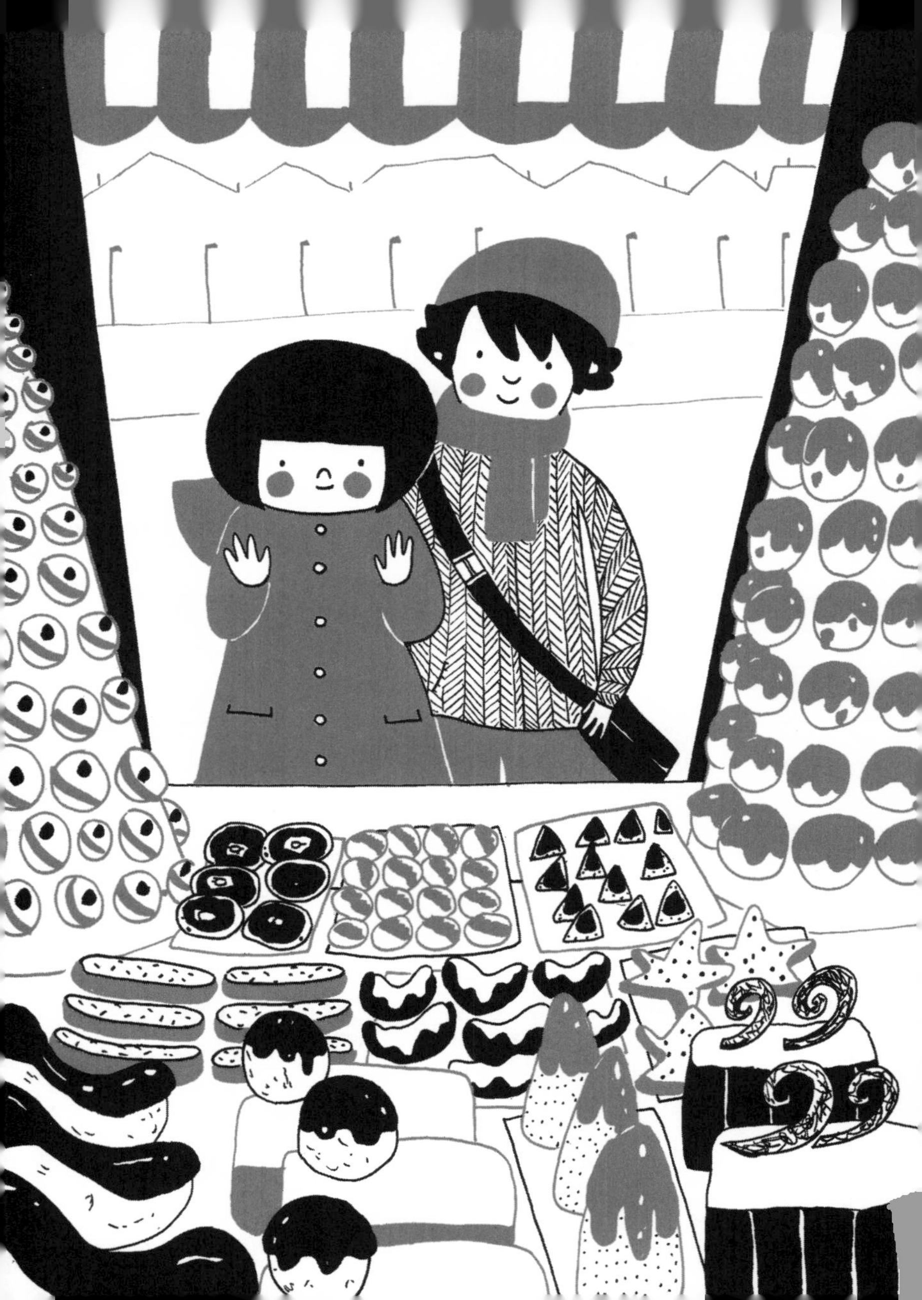

Your new phone still has the default wallpaper
I'll make you one
DON'T LOOK!
lovely

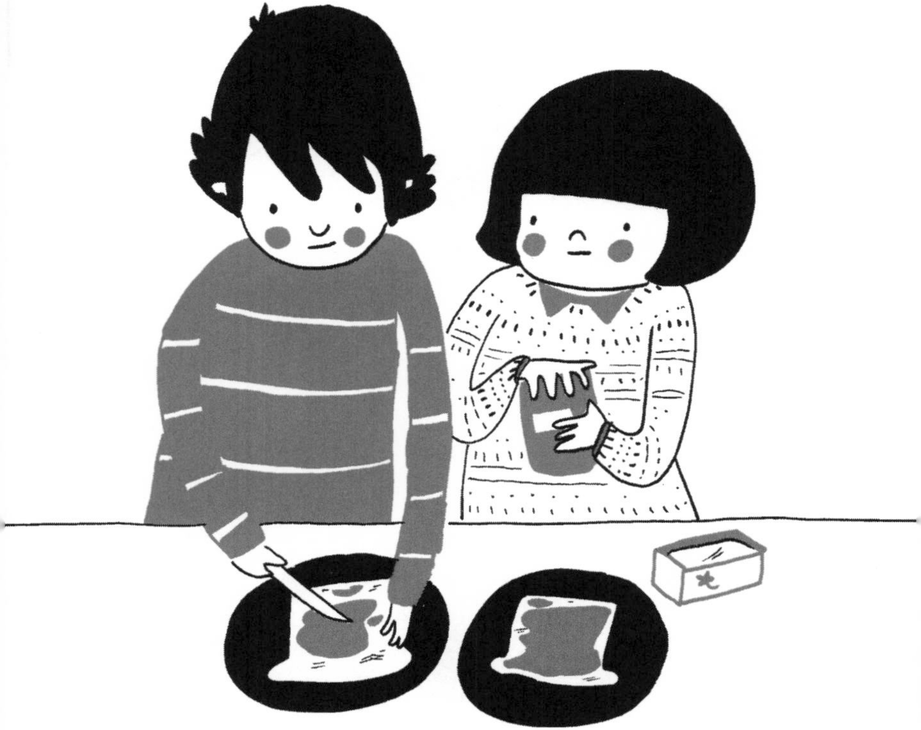

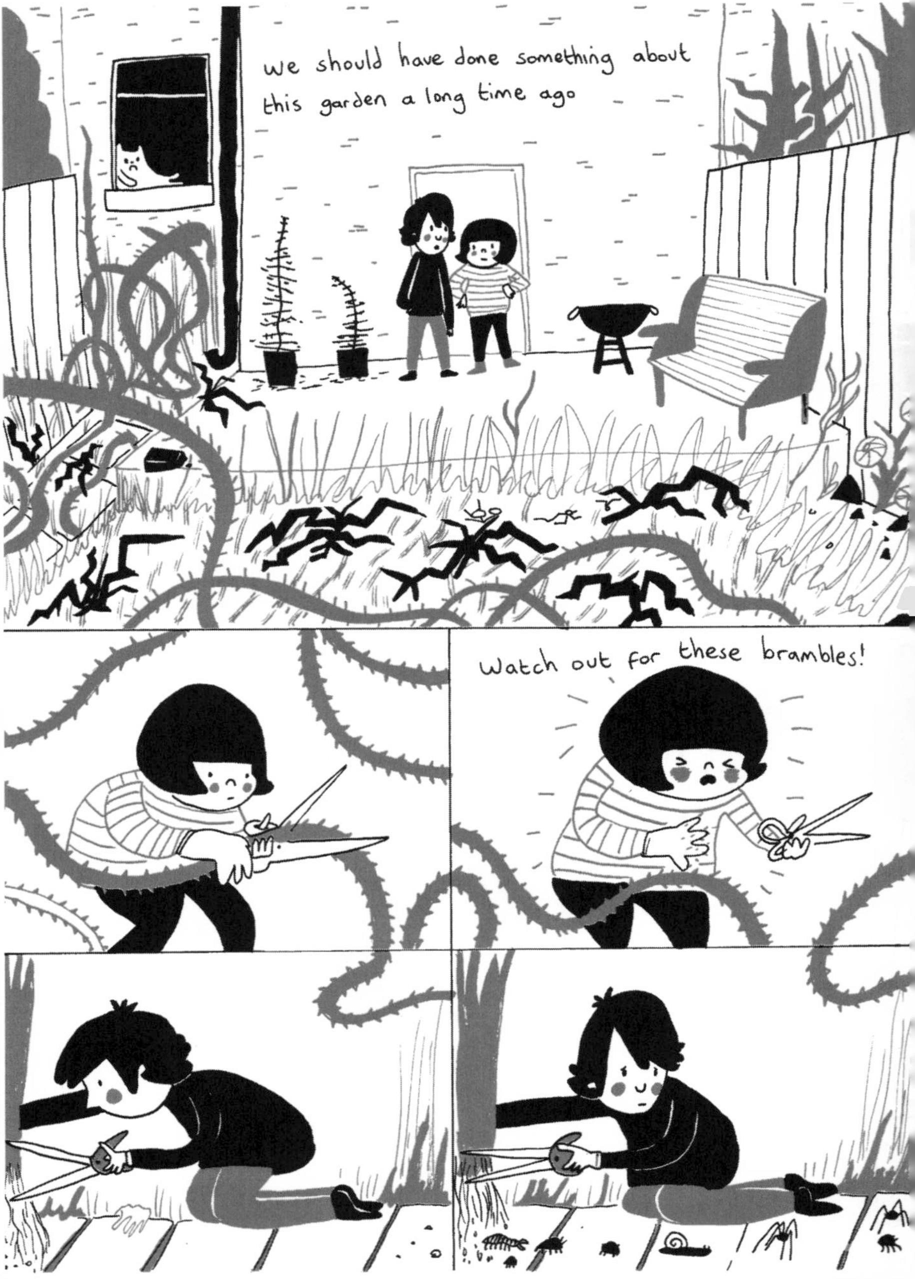
we should have done something about this garden a long time ago
Watch out for these brambles!

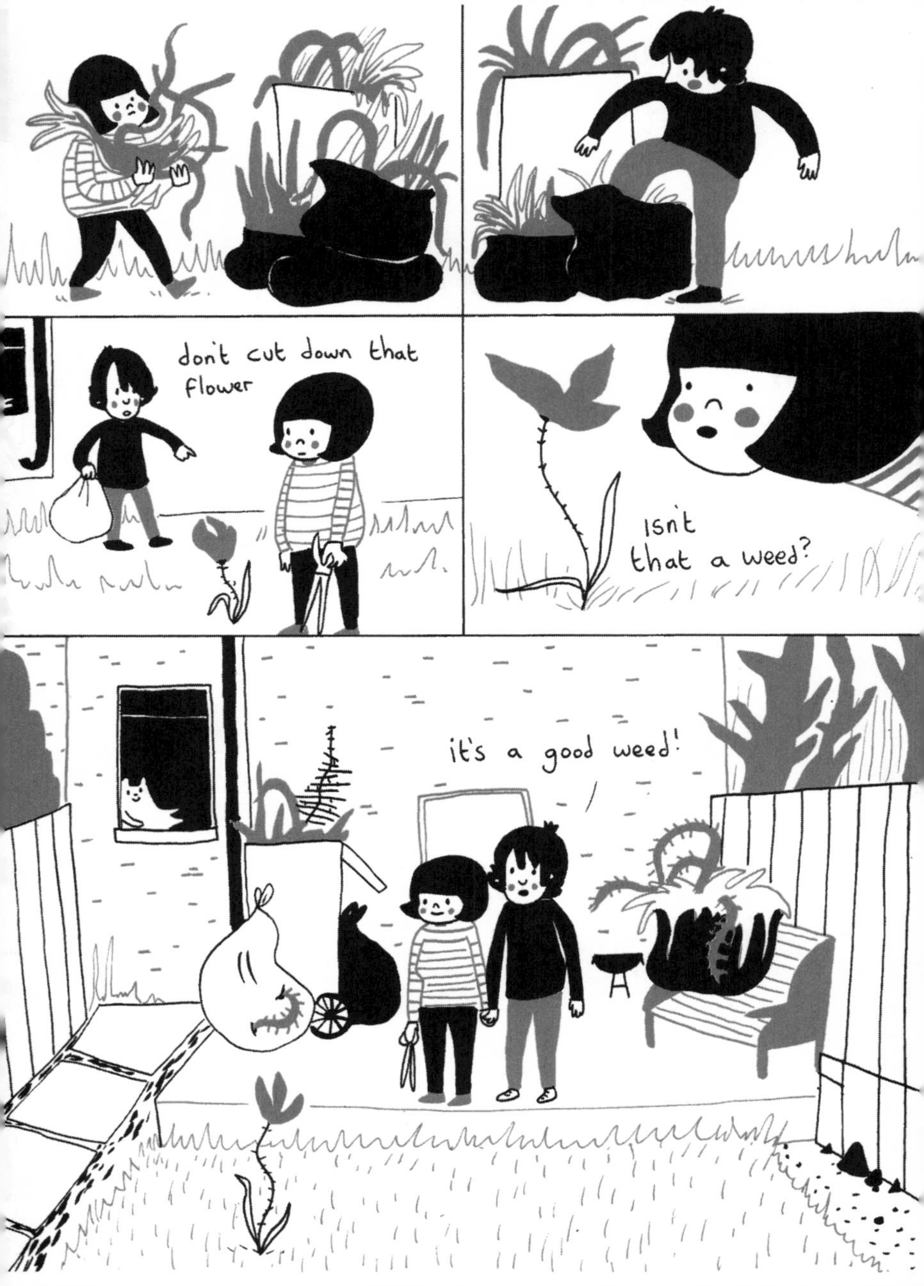
don't cut down that flower
isn't that a weed?
it's a good weed!

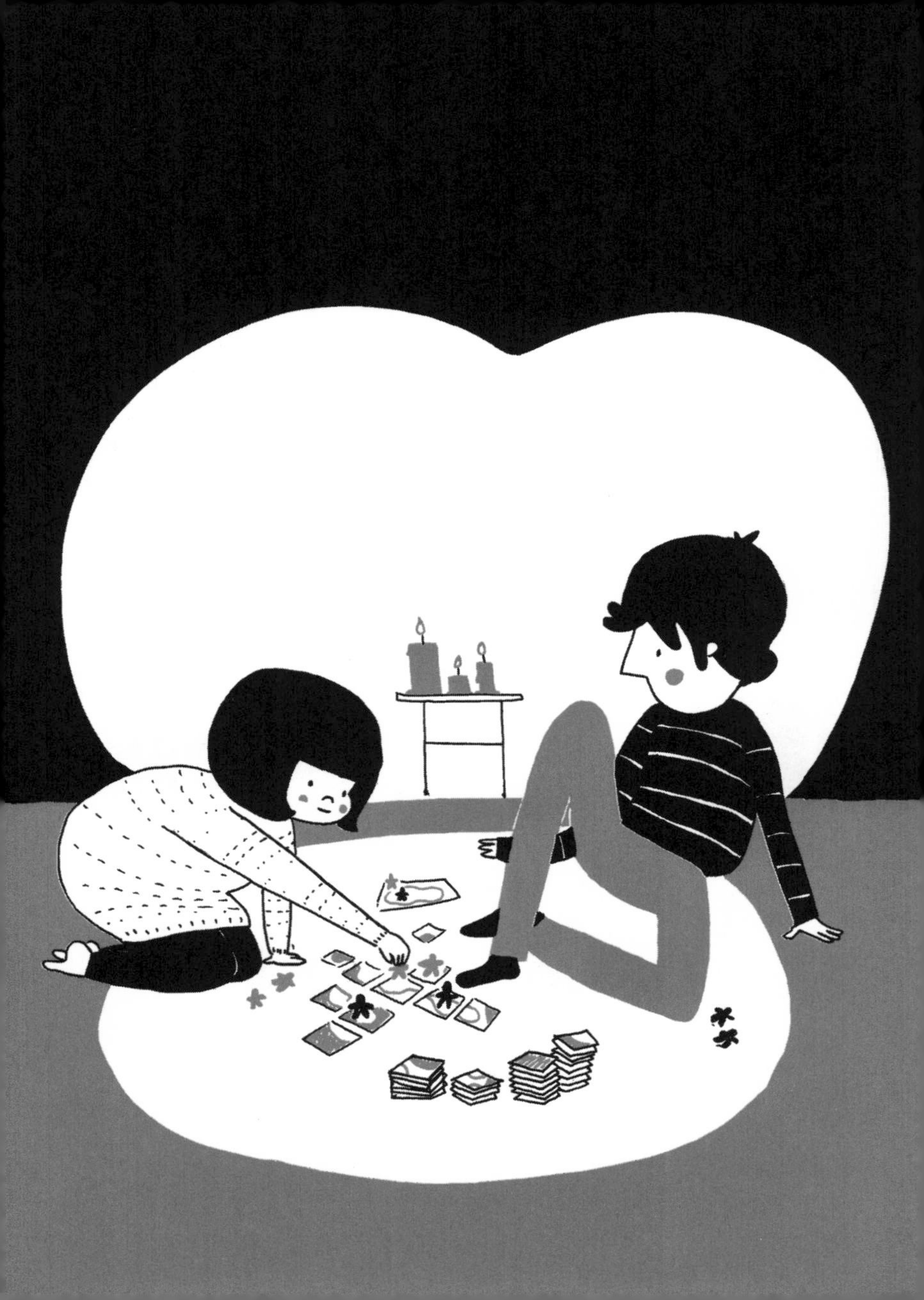

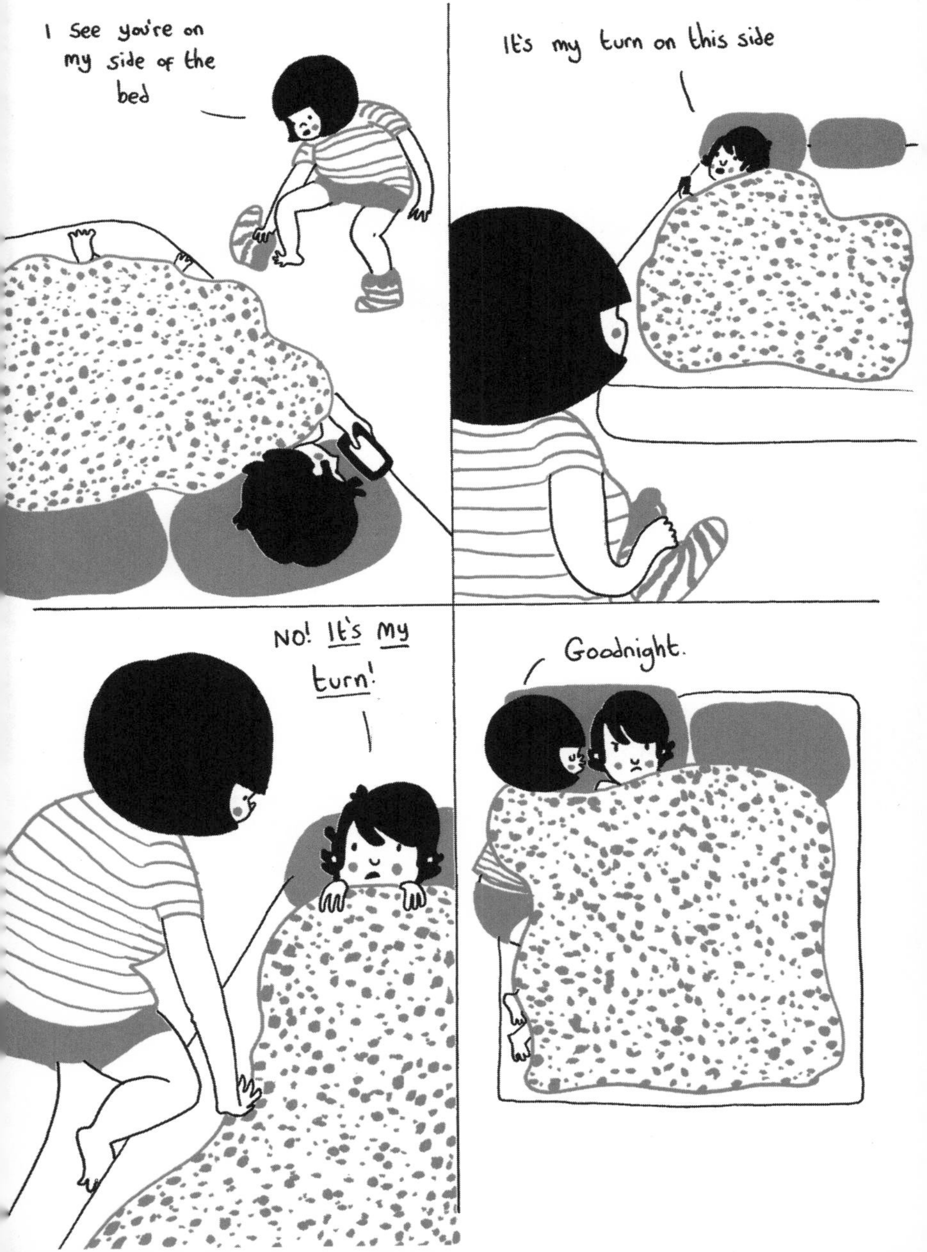
I see you're on my side of the bed
It's my turn on this side
No! It's my turn!
Goodnight.

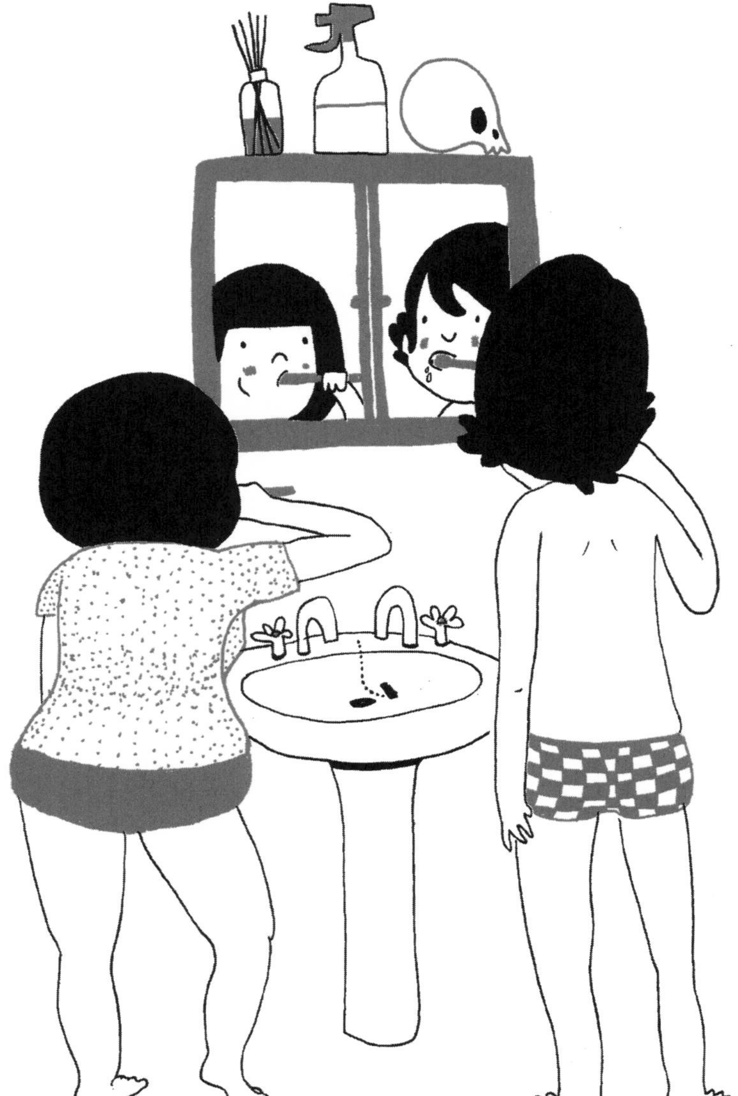

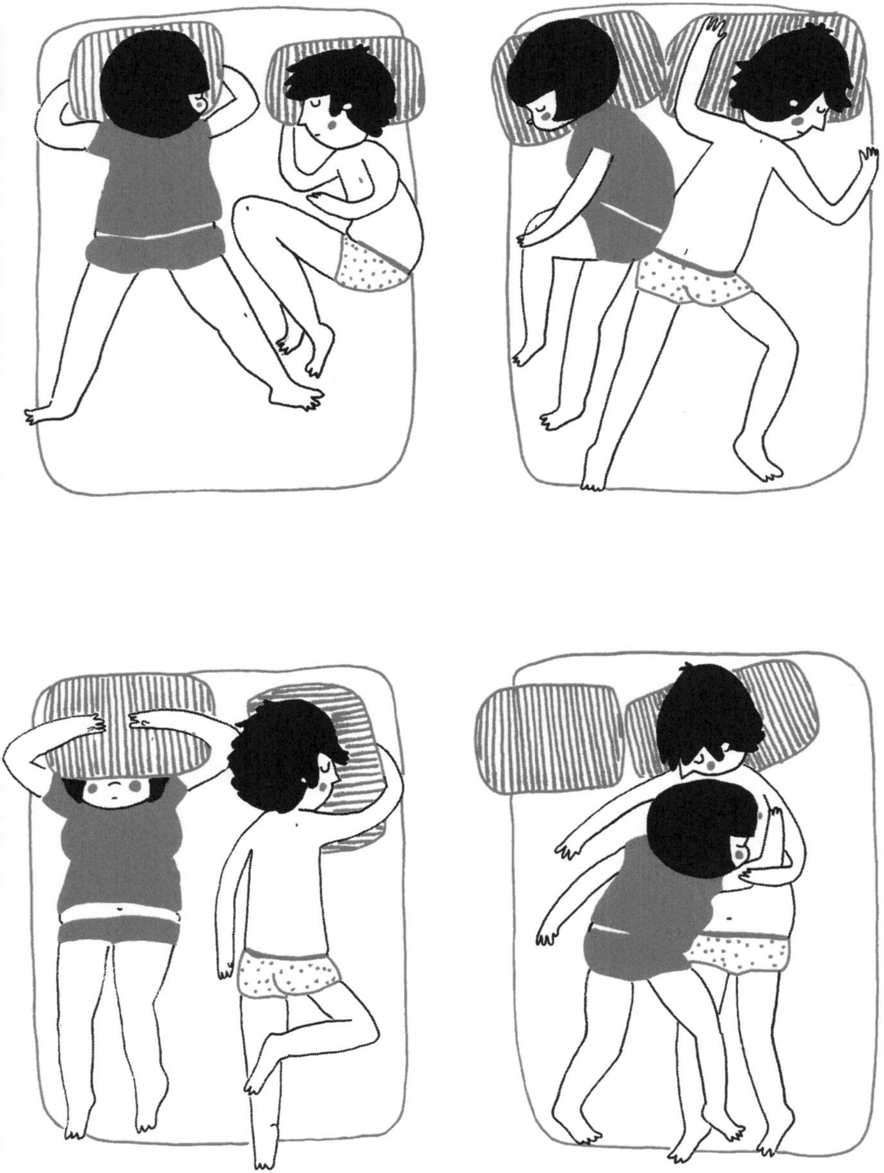

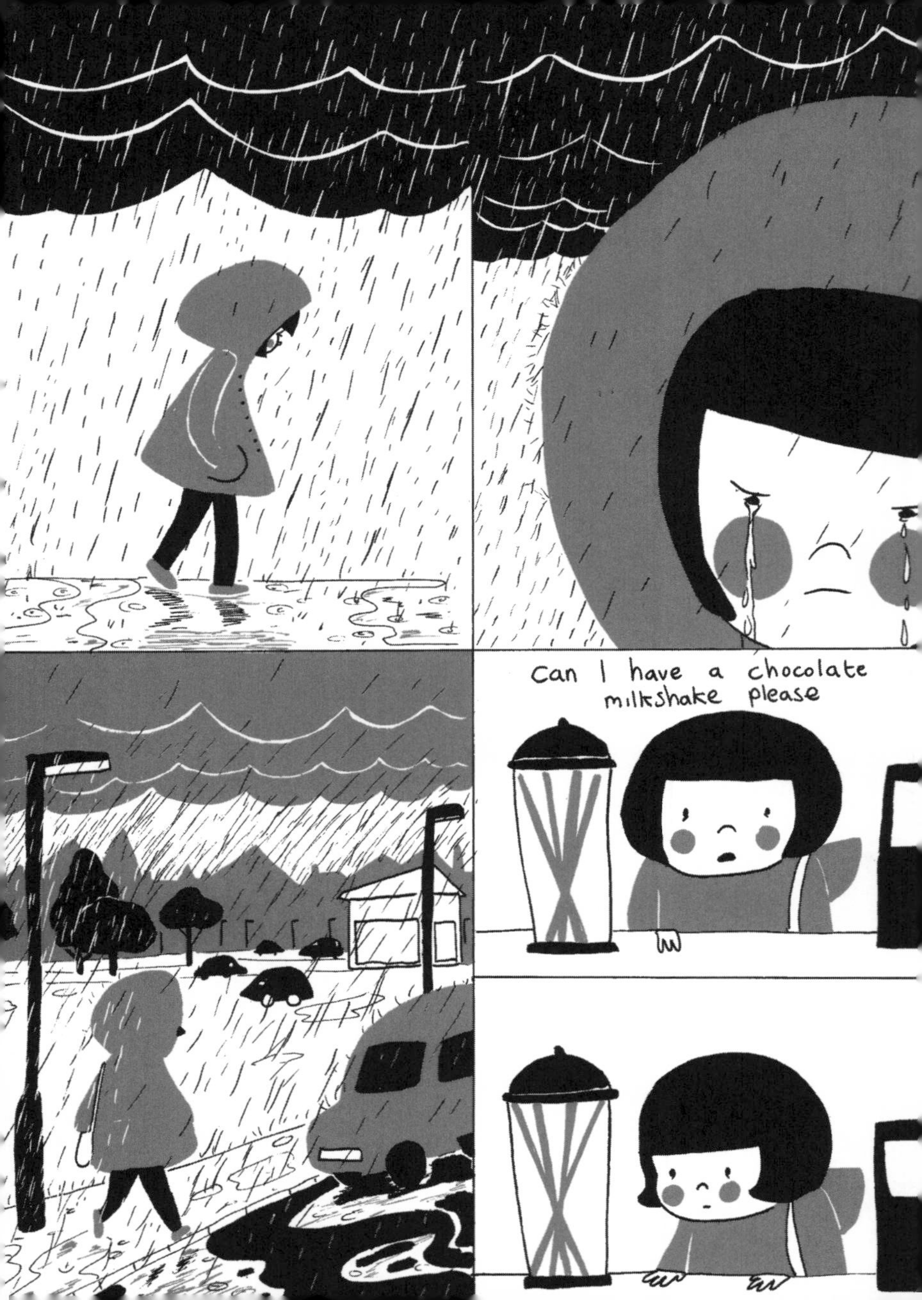
Can I have a chocolate milkshake please

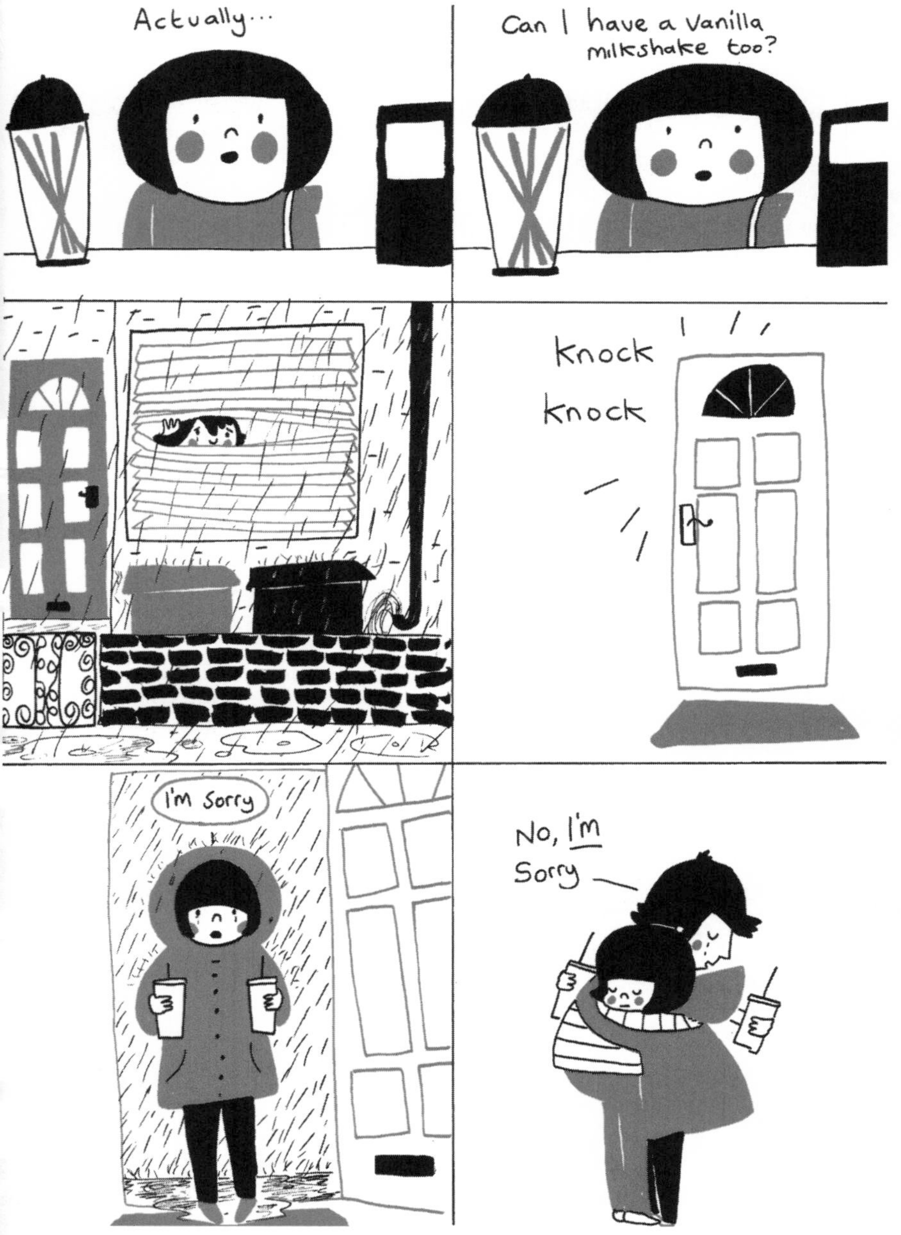
Actually...
Can I have a vanilla milkshake too?
knock
knock
I'm Sorry
No, I'm Sorry

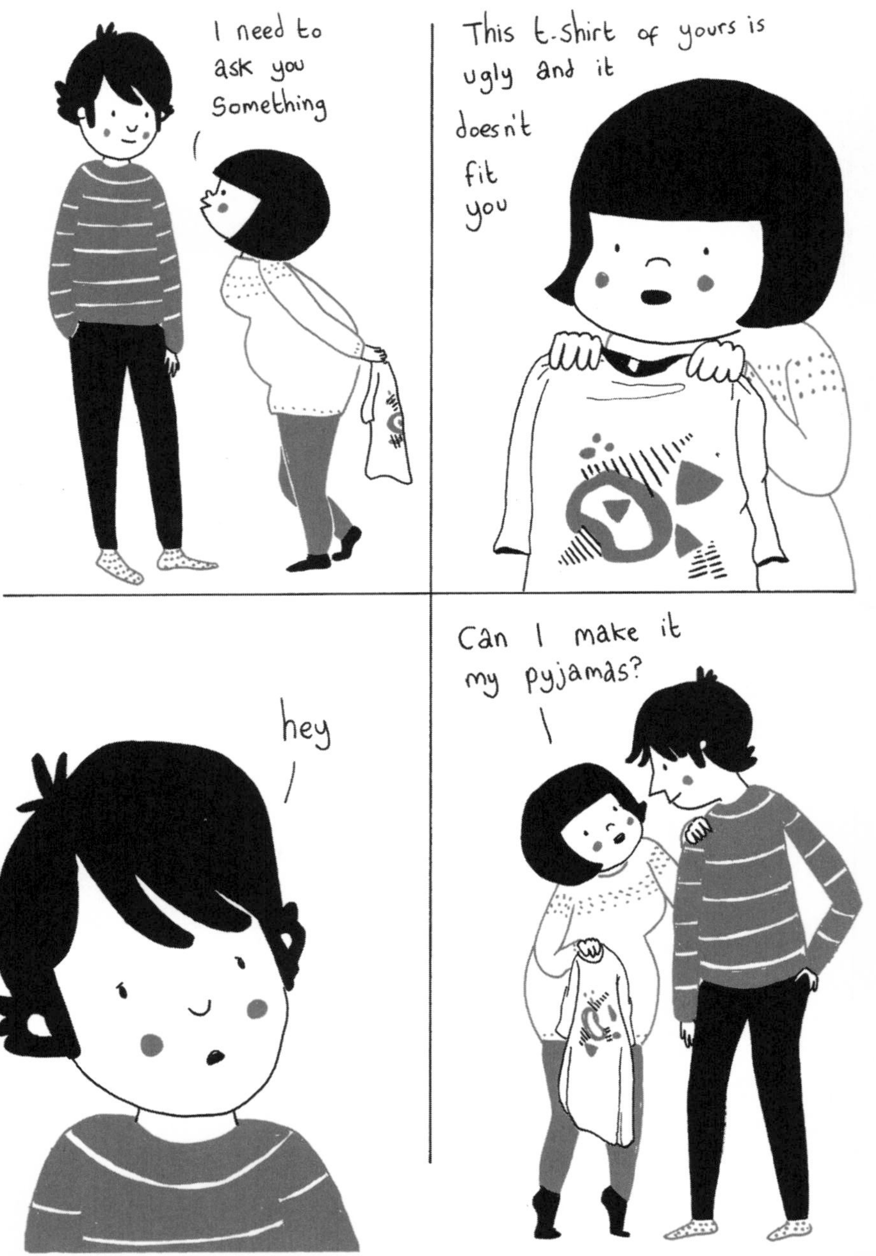
I need to ask you Something
This t-shirt of yours is ugly and it doesn't fit you
hey
Can I make it my pyjamas?

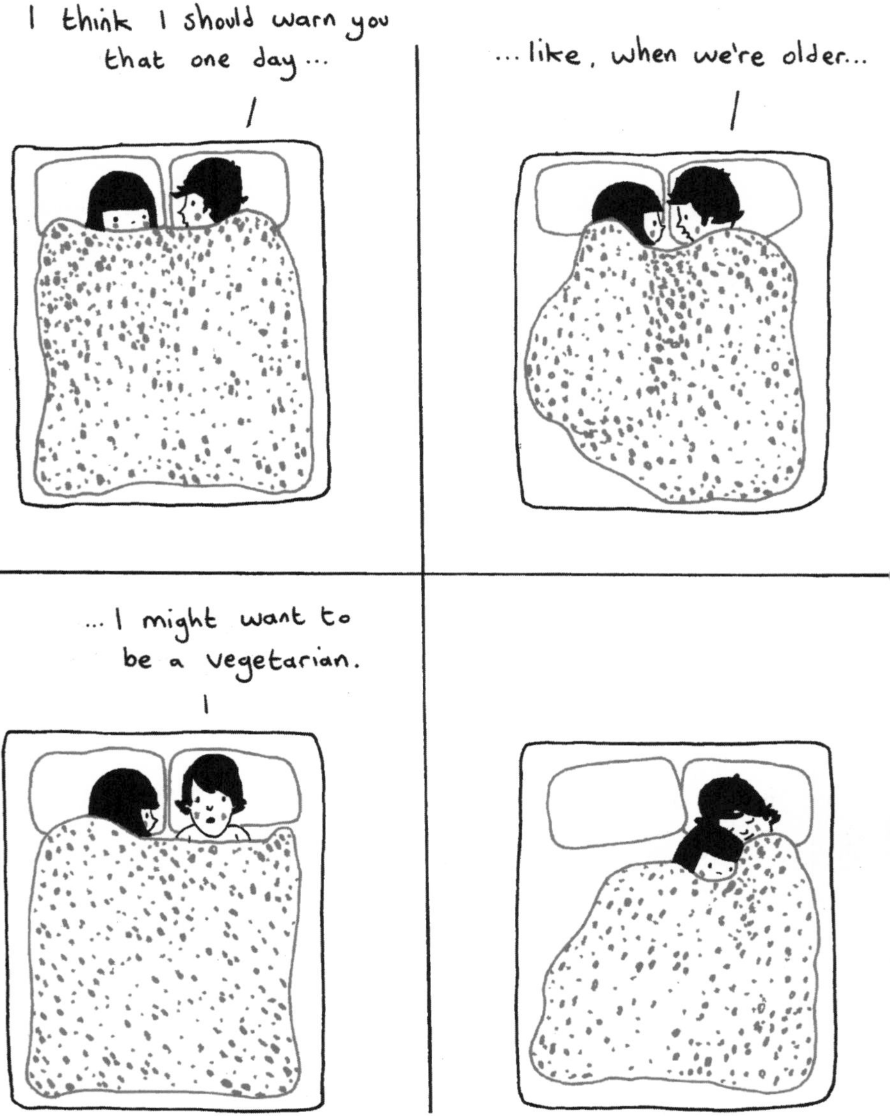
I think I should warn you that one day...
...like, when we're older...
...I might want to be a vegetarian.

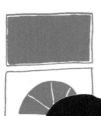

Are you ready?

Yes, except my scarf

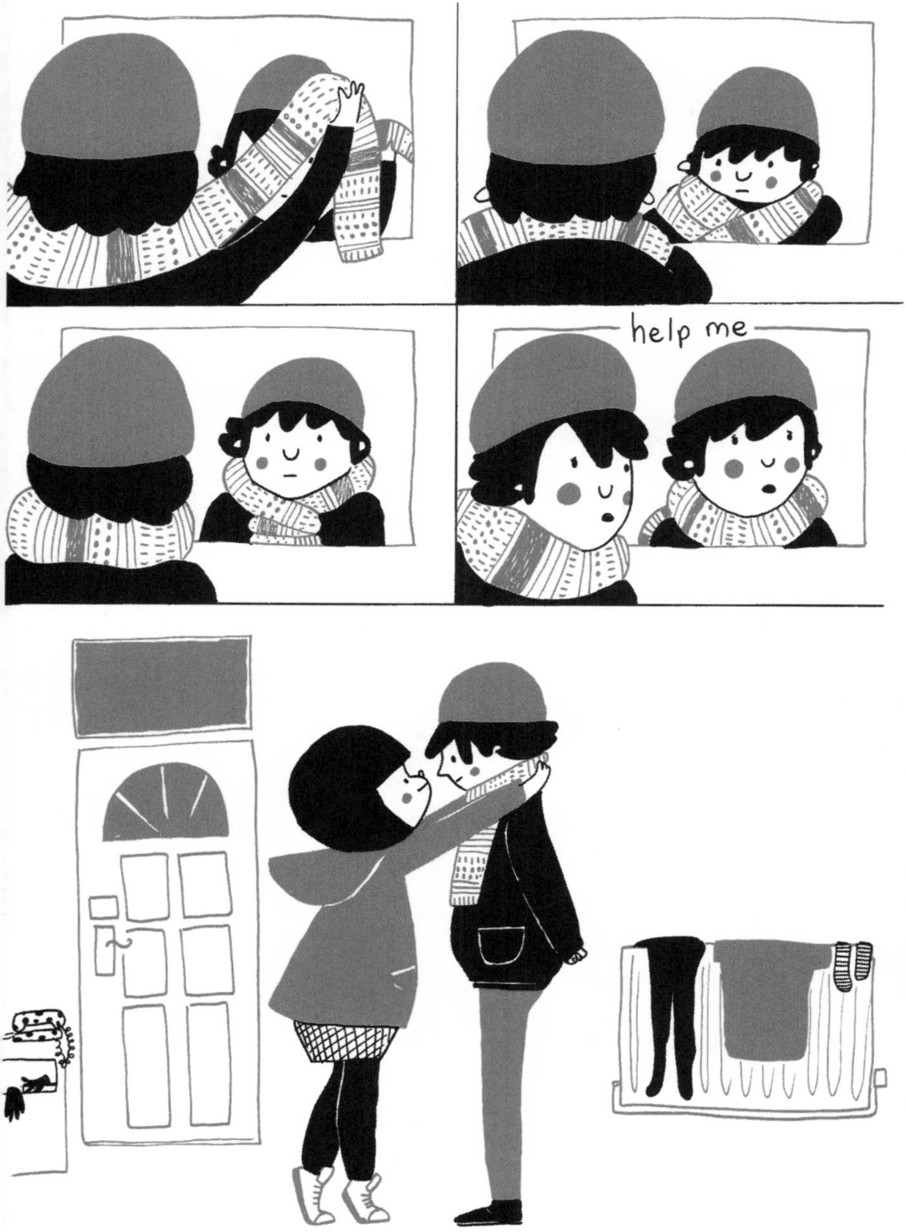
help me

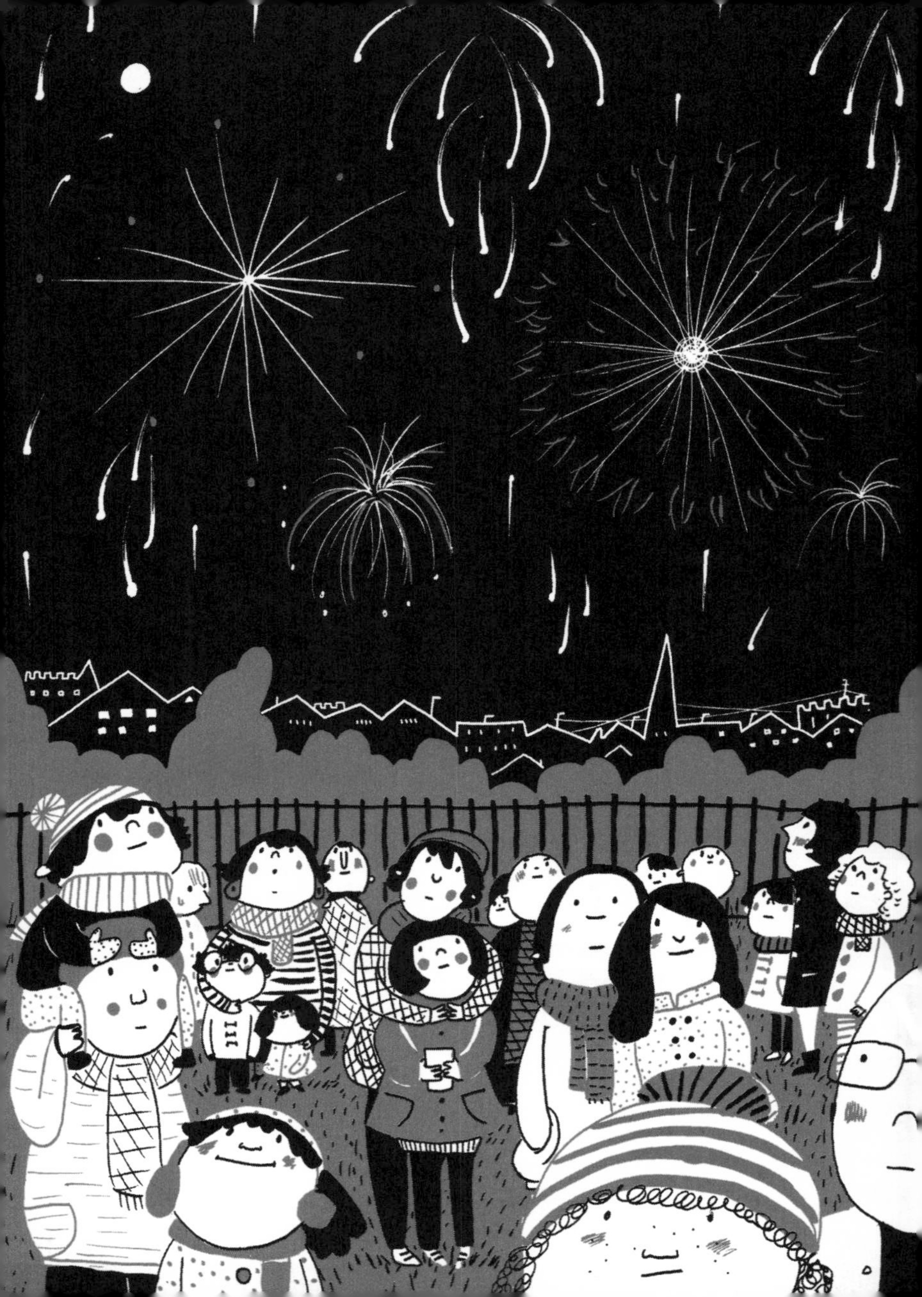

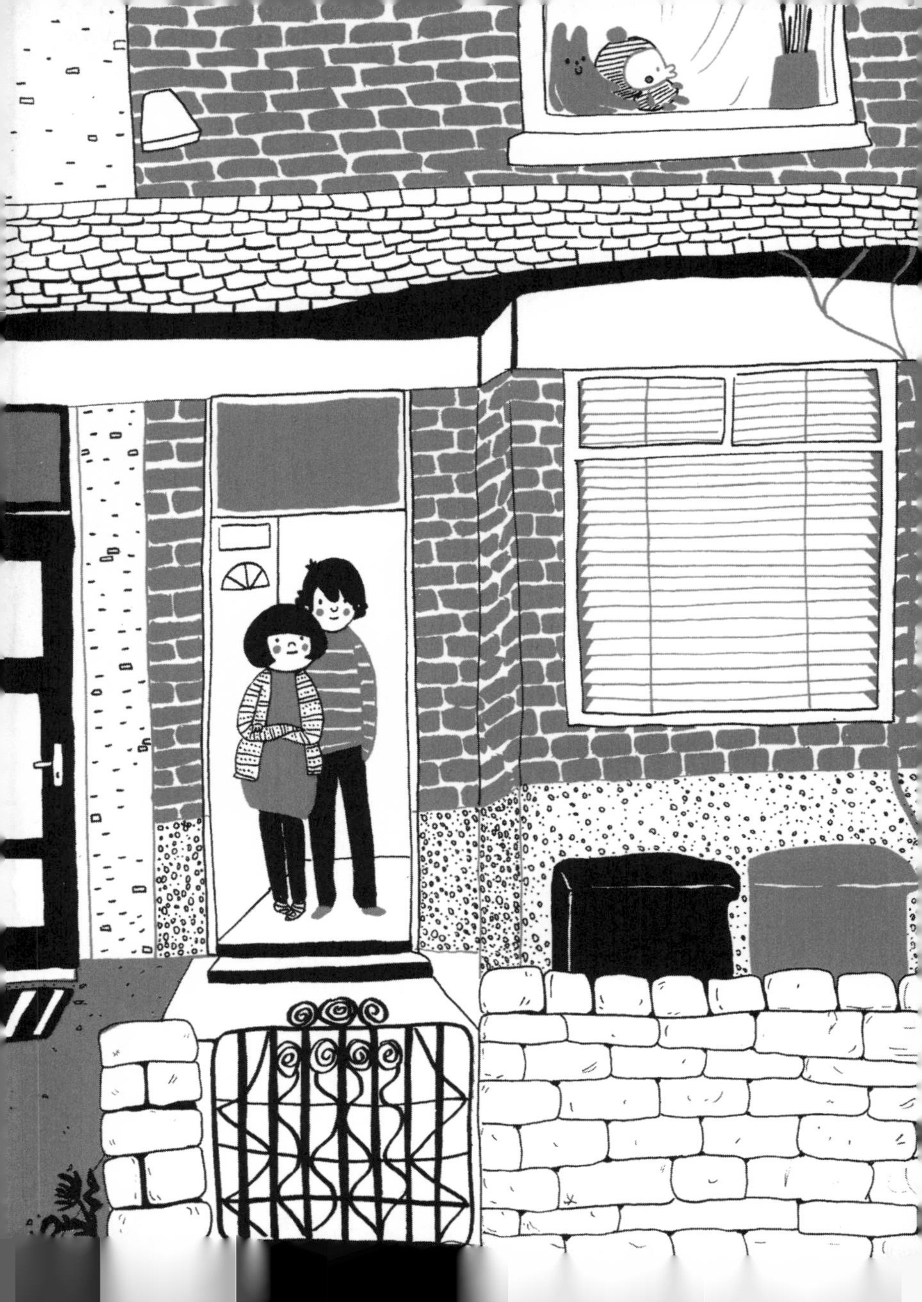

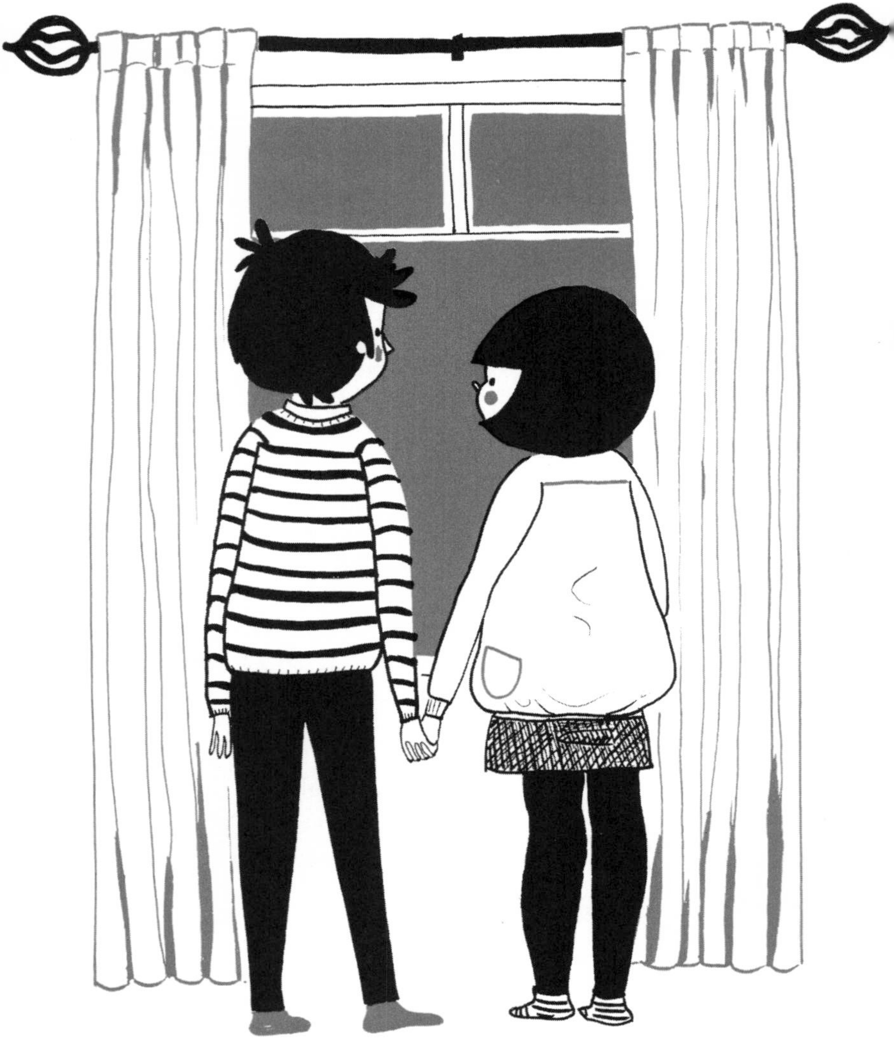